Charles H. Walsh

Patriotic and Naval Songster

Charles H. Walsh

Patriotic and Naval Songster

ISBN/EAN: 9783337265489

Printed in Europe, USA, Canada, Australia, Japan

Cover: Foto ©Thomas Meinert / pixelio.de

More available books at **www.hansebooks.com**

PATRIOTIC

AND

NAVAL

SONGSTER

"Sail on, O Ship of State!
Sail on, O Union, strong and great!
Humanity, with all its fears,
With all the hopes of future years,
Is hanging, breathless, on thy fate!
* * * *
Sail on, nor fear to breast the sea!
Our hearts, our hopes, our prayers, our tears,
Our faith, triumphant o'er our fears,
Are all with thee,—are all with thee."

LONGFELLOW.

CHARLES H. WALSH

1037 WALNUT STREET, PHILADELPHIA

1898

Pour forth a full libation now
  To Farragut the brave—
The idol of the Navy and
  The ruler of the Wave.
He's gone aloft, lashed in his shroud,
  Where soon we all must go;
He's waiting there to welcome us
  With Benny Havens, oh!
                (General James McQuade.)

PREFACE.

"Dulce et decorum est pro patria mori."

Of the many instances illustrative of the influence of song, as a moral force, we have selected the following as one of the most pertinent :—

"A day or two after Lee's surrender in April, 1865," writes a contributor to the *Century Magazine*, "I left our ship at 'Dutch Gap,' in the James River, for a run up to Richmond, where I was joined by the ship's surgeon, the paymaster, and one of the junior officers. After 'doing' Richmond pretty thoroughly, we went in the evening to my rooms for dinner. Dinner being over and the events of the day recounted, the doctor, who was a fine player, opened the piano, saying : 'Boys, we've got our old quartette here ; let's have a song.' As the house opposite was occupied by paroled Confederate officers, no patriotic songs were sung. Soon the lady of the house handed me this note : ' Compliments of General——— and Staff. Will the gentlemen kindly allow us to come over and hear them sing?' Of course we consented, and they came. As the general entered the room, I recognized instantly the face and figure of one who stood second only to Lee or Jackson in the whole Confederacy. After introductions and the usual interchange of civilities, we sang for them glees and college songs, until at last the general said : 'Excuse me, gentlemen, you sing delightfully, but what *we* want to hear is your army songs.' Then we gave them the army songs with unction, the 'Battle Hymn of the Republic,' 'John Brown's Body,' 'We're Coming, Father Abraham,' 'Tramp, Tramp, Tramp, the Boys are Marching,' through the whole catalogue, to the 'Star-Spangled Banner,'—to which many a foot beat time as if it had never stepped to any but the 'music of the Union,'—and closed our concert with 'Rally Round the Flag, Boys.' When the applause had subsided, a tall, fine-looking fellow in a major's uniform exclaimed, 'Gentlemen, if we'd had your songs we'd have licked you out of your boots ! Who couldn't have marched or fought with such songs? We had nothing, absolutely nothing, except a bastard 'Marseillaise,' the 'Bonny Blue Flag,' and 'Dixie,' which were nothing but jigs. 'Maryland, my

Maryland' was a splendid song, but the true, old 'Lauriger Horatius' was about as inspiring as the 'Dead March in Saul,' while every one of these Yankee songs is full of marching and fighting spirit.' Then turning to the general he said: 'I shall never forget the first time I heard "Rally Round the Flag." 'Twas a nasty night during the "Seven Days' Fight," and if I remember rightly it was raining. I was on picket, when, just before "taps," some fellow on the other side struck up that song and others joined in the chorus until it seemed to me the whole Yankee army was singing. Tom B———, who was with me, sung out, "Good heavens, Cap, what are those fellows made of, anyway? Here we've licked 'em six days running and now, on the eve of the seventh, they're singing 'Rally Round the Flag.'" I am not naturally superstitious, but I tell you that song sounded to me like the "knell of doom," and my heart went down into my boots; and though I've tried to do my duty, it has been an up-hill fight with me ever since that night.'"

The object of making this collection of songs was not merely to furnish a means of amusement. There was a higher motive— Lyric poetry is, in a certain sense, history, "the most profitable of all studies." Through many of these songs may be traced something of the history of our country and of its Navy.

There was a still higher motive. Nothing so thoroughly implants, in the breasts of the young, a love for, and a devotion to, the flag, and to the country it symbolizes, as the songs, however rude, recounting the brave deeds of the heroes who laid, and of those who have built upon, the foundations of our national glory.

That this collection of Patriotic, Naval, and Sea Songs, deficient though it be in literary merit, may serve to inspire the youth of America with an ardent sense of patriotism, is the earnest hope of

THE PUBLISHER.

The Publisher acknowledges with thanks the courtesy of Messrs. Wm. A. Pond & Co., in permitting the use of their excellent edition of Naval Songs.

Patriotic and Naval Songster.

Hail, Columbia.

(JOSEPH HOPKINSON, 1798.)

Hail, Columbia, happy land! hail, ye heroes, heaven-born band
    Who fought and bled in Freedom's cause,
    Who fought and bled in Freedom's cause,
And when the storm of war was gone, enjoyed the peace your valor won.
Let independence be our boast, ever mindful what it cost;
Ever grateful for the prize, let its altar reach the skies.

    CHORUS.

Firm, united let us be, rallying round our liberty;
As a band of brothers joined, peace and safety we shall find.

Immortal patriots! rise once more—defend your rights, defend your shore;
    Let no rude foe, with impious hand,
    Let no rude foe, with impious hand,
Invade the shrine where sacred lies, of toil and blood, the well-earned prize,
While offering peace, sincere and just, in heaven we place a manly trust,
That truth and justice will prevail, and every scheme of bondage fail.

    CHORUS—Firm, united let us be, &c.

Sound, sound the trumpet of fame! let Washington's great name
        Ring through the world with loud applause,
        Ring through the world with loud applause,
Let every clime to Freedom dear, listen with a joyful ear,
With equal skill and god-like power, he governs in the fearful hour
Of horrid war; or guides, with ease, the happier times of honest
    peace.
        CHORUS – Firm, united let us be, &c.

Behold the chief who now commands, again to serve his country,
    stands
        The rock on which the storm will beat,
        The rock on which the storm will beat;
But, armed in virtue, firm and true, his hopes are fixed on heaven
    and you
When hope was sinking in dismay, and gloom obscured Columbia's
    day,
His steady mind, from changes free, resolved on death or liberty.

        CHORUS—Firm, united let us be, &c.

The Star-Spangled Banner.

(FRANCIS SCOTT KEY, Sept. 14th, 1814.)

O! say, can you see, by the dawn's early light,
    What so proudly we hailed at the twilight's last gleaming:
Whose broad stripes and bright stars, through the perilous fight,
    O'er the ramparts we watched were so gallantly streaming.
And the rocket's red glare, the bombs bursting in air,
    Gave proof through the night that our flag was still there;

        O! say, does the Star-spangled Banner still wave
        O'er the land of the free and the home of the brave?

On the shore, dimly seen through the mist of the deep,
  Where the foe's haughty host in dread silence reposes,
What is that which the breeze, o'er the towering steep,
  As it fitfully blows, half conceals, half discloses?
Now it catches the gleam of the morning's first beam—
  In full glory reflected, now shines on the stream;

    'Tis the Star-spangled Banner, O! long may it wave
    O'er the land of the free and the home of the brave.

And where is the band who so vauntingly swore
  That the havoc of war and the battle's confusion
A home and a country would leave us no more?
  Their blood has wash'd out their foul footstep's pollution.
No refuge could save the hireling and slave
  From the terror of flight or the gloom of the grave!

    And the Star-spangled Banner in triumph doth wave
    O'er the land of the free and the home of the brave.

O! thus be it ever when freemen shall stand
  Between their lov'd homes and the foe's desolation;
Bless'd with victory and peace, may our Heaven-rescued land
  Praise the Power that hath made and preserved us a nation.
Then conquer we must, for our cause it is just—
  And this be our motto—" In God is our trust!"

    And the Star-spangled Banner in triumph shall wave
    O'er the land of the free and the home of the brave.

    (Additional Verse by DR. O. W. HOLMES.)

When our land is illum'd with liberty's smile,
  If a foe from within strike a blow at her glory,
Down, down with the traitor, that dares to defile
  The flag of her stars and the page of her story!
By the millions unchain'd who our birthright have gained
  We will keep her bright blazon forever unstained!

    And the Star-spangled Banner in triumph shall wave
    While the land of the free is the home of the brave!

America.

(DR. S. F. SMITH, 1831.)

My country, 'tis of thee,
Sweet land of liberty,
  Of thee I sing;
Land where my father died,
Land of the pilgrims' pride,
From every mountain side,
  Let freedom ring.

My native country, thee,
Land of the noble, free—
  Thy name I love;
I love thy rocks and rills,
Thy woods and templed hills;
My heart with rapture thrills
  Like that above.

Let music swell the breeze,
And ring from all the trees,
  Sweet freedom's song;
Let mortal tongues awake,
Let all that breathe partake,
Let rocks their silence break,
  The sound prolong.

Our fathers' God, to Thee,
Author of liberty,
  To Thee I sing;
Long may our land be bright
With freedom's holy light;
Protect us by Thy might,
  Great God, our King.

God Save the Flag!

(O. W. HOLMES, 1865.)

Washed in the blood of the brave and the blooming,
   Snatched from the altars of insolent foes,
Burning with star-fires, but never consuming,
   Flash its broad ribbons of lily and rose.

Vainly the prophets of Baal would rend it,
   Vainly his worshipers pray for its fall;
Thousands have died for it, millions defend it,
   Emblem of justice and mercy to all:

Justice that reddens the sky with her terrors,
   Mercy that comes with her white-handed train,
Soothing all passions, redeeming all errors,
   Sheathing the sabre and breaking the chain.

Borne on the deluge of old usurpations,
   Drifted our Ark o'er the desolate seas;
Bearing the rainbow of hope to the nations,
   Torn from the storm-cloud and flung to the breeze!

God bless the Flag and its loyal defenders,
   While its broad folds o'er the battle-field wave,
Till the dim star-wreath rekindle its splendors,
   Washed from its stains in the blood of the brave!

The Battle Hymn of the Republic.

MRS. JULIA WARD HOWE.

Mine eyes have seen the glory of the coming of the Lord;
He is trampling out the vintage where the grapes of wrath are
    stored.
He hath loosed the fateful lightning of His terrible swift sword;
    His truth is marching on.

I have seen Him in the watch-fires of a hundred circling camps;
They have builded Him an altar in the evening dews and damps.
I have read His righteous sentence by the dim and flaring lamps:
      His day is marching on.

I have read a fiery gospel writ in burnished rows of steel:
"As ye deal with my contemners, so with you My grace shall deal:
Let the hero, born of woman, crush the serpent with his heel,
      Since God is marching on."

He has sounded forth the trumpet that shall never call retreat;
He is sifting out the hearts of men before His judgment-seat:
Oh, be swift, my soul, to answer Him,—be jubilant, my feet!
      Our God is marching on.

In the beauty of the lilies Christ was born across the sea,
With a glory in His bosom that transfigures you and me:
As He died to make men holy, let us die to make men free,
      While God is marching on.

"First in Peace, First in War, and First in the Hearts of his Countrymen."

The Nation's Heritage.

The years flow on, a mighty stream,
And stars of Genius o'er it gleam!
Alas! those stars oft fade and die,
And shine no more upon the sky.

But in that temple bright of Fame
There dwells a hallowed, deathless name,
A talisman to Valor's might,
The Hero's shield and sword of Right!

Oh, natal day for patriot's dreams
Where'er our starlit banner streams!
Recall the past — its glorious worth —
E'en now re-echoed 'round the earth!

As lightning to dark skies of night
That name pierced through the tyrant's blight!
A hope for nations yet to be —
God sent through all eternity!

In heart of hearts that name shall thrill,
And nerve each patriot's arms and will!
And beacon like a guiding star
The struggling souls of realms afar!

Oh, Fame undying, pure and great!
Oh, Worth for men to emulate!
Oh, Patriot heart, earth's glory won,
Time keeps thy name, oh, Washington!
—*New York Clipper.*

When Freedom's Star Its Last Bright Gleam.

1817.

[Air: "Rule Britannia."]

When freedom's star its last bright gleam,
  O'er Europe's waste had shot in vain,
Columbia caught the expiring beam,
  And bore it o'er the western main.

    Rule Columbia, Columbia ever free,
    Heaven-born child of liberty.

Then rose a world, by Heaven's decree,
  Which countless years unblest had lain,
But now the destin'd sphere to be,
  Of Freedom's pure and sacred reign.
    Rule Columbia, &c.

Then ere Columbia thou hadst shar'd,
  Of empire's car the trembling reign,
Thy young but dauntless soul declar'd,
  War's storms but threaten thee in vain.
    Rule Columbia, &c.

And when ere long, with step-dame pride,
  Britannia mark'd thy opening reign,
Thy Heaven-shielded breast defied
  The tempest shock of war again.
    Rule Columbia, &c.

Thy birth, Columbia, sons so brave,
  Thy waters, forests, all proclaim
Thy destin'd course is o'er the wave,
  And ocean is thy "field of fame."
    Rule Columbia, &c.

Again behold war's bolts are hurl'd,
  Thy eagle flight to check in vain,
For still thy infant flag unfurl'd
  With freedom's charter sweeps the main.
    Rule Columbia, &c.

And under Heaven it still shall spread,
  Its star-gemm'd glories o'er the main,
While freedom's sacred beam shall shed,
  Its light to bless Columbia's reign.
    Rule Columbia, Columbia ever free,
    Heaven-born child of liberty.

Whene'er the Tyrants of the Main.

1817.

[Air: "Mrs. Casey."]

Whene'er the tyrants of the main
  Assault Columbian seamen,
They'll find them ready to maintain
  The noble name of *Freemen*.

CHORUS.

  Then toast the brave, for they will save
    Columbia's fame from sinking;
  The honor'd scars of *Yankee Tars*
    Are glorious themes for drinking.

Too long our tars have borne, in peace,
  With British domineering;
But now they've sworn the trade shall cease—
  For vengeance they are steering.

    Then toast, &c.

First gallant HULL, he was the lad,
  Who sailed a tyrant-hunting,
And swaggering Dacres soon was glad
  To strike to "*striped bunting!*"

    Then toast, &c.

Intrepid JONES next boldly sought
  The demons of oppression:
With a superior force he fought,
  And gave the knaves a thrashing.

    Then toast, &c.

Then quickly met our nation's eyes
   The noblest sight in nature—
A first-rate frigate as a *prize*,
   Brought in by brave DECATUR.
      Then toast, &c.

The veteran BAINBRIDGE next prepared
   To wield his country's thunder;
In quest of foes, he boldly steered,
   And drove the *Java* under.
      Then toast, &c.

And daring LAWRENCE next parades,
   From zone to zone he sought 'em:
One boasting Briton he blockades,
   And sends one to the bottom.
      Then toast, &c.

Next see our gallant *Enterprise*,
   How nobly ocean rocks her!
There BURROWS for his country dies,
   But first subdues the *Boxer*.
      Then toast, &c.

With loud applause next we greet
   The glorious news from *Erie*,
Behold! a powerful British fleet
   Submits to gallant PERRY.
      Then toast, &c.

Then WARRINGTON, his country's pride,
   Sails boldly forth to serve her;
And quickly humbled by his side,
   We see the fierce *Epervier!*
      Then toast, &c.

From noble BLAKELY'S dauntless force,
  His vanquished foes in vain steer :
For he could stop the *Avon's* course,
  And overhaul the *Reindeer !*

    Then toast, &c.

M'DONOUGH ! hero of Champlain,
  Next proved that British seamen
With *Yankee Tars* contend in vain—
  Because those tars are *Freemen.*

    Then toast, &c.

With " Ironsides," brave STEWART slips
  To sea, on her *third* cruise, sir,
And tired of flogging *single* ships.
  She drubs them now by *two's*, sir !

    Then toast, &c.

The *Penguin* next, with her vain crew,
  Thought she to strike, would scorn it :
She sought a *Wasp*—but found in lieu,
  Our BIDDLE, and his *Hornet !*

    Then toast, &c.

Our *Yankee Tars*, to Afric's shores,
  Our Heroes lastly lead 'em —
And Turkish banners bow before
  The starry flag of freedom.

    Then toast, &c.

Come push the flowing bowl around,
  And in Columbia's story,
Long may such gallant names abound,
  To vindicate her glory !

    Then toast the brave, for they will save
      Columbia's fame from sinking ;
    The honor'd scars of *Yankee Tars*
      Are glorious themes for drinking.

The Wave of Old Ocean's the Field for the Brave.

1817.

[Air: " Thy Blue Waves O'Carron "]

"The wave of old Ocean's the field for the brave,"
  "D'ye see, Jack, thus says the old song as it goes,
And somehow or other, if one meets a grave,
  Why it comes in the shape of our country's foes.
And to die in the cause of mankind and our own,
  Is the pride and the joy of a true-hearted tar;
While the cherub of light sweetly sings his renown,
  Which flies to the land of his home from afar."

'Twas thus as we swung in our hammocks one night,
  Tom Junk to his messmates so gallantly spake;
We heard him with joy, and our bosoms beat light,
  In the hope that we stood in the enemy's wake.
Next day was the battle, our foes they were bold,
  But American sailors to conquer were sworn;
And tho' fiercely the tide of the conflict was roll'd,
  The wreath from the brow of Britannia was torn.

In the midst of the fight, when the scuppers ran blood,
  Bold Tom, like a lion, the contest maintain'd,
At his gun, undismayed and collected he stood,
  While the bullets on deck like a wild tempest rain'd.
He stood at his gun with a soul so serene,
  That he jested and laugh'd to messmates around;
But the moment that victory lightened the scene,
  He fell, like the oak, in full majesty crown'd.

He fell—but the soul of the sailor was strong,
  His eyes to the flag of Columbia arose,
And he smil'd to his friends, as it floated along
  From the top of the conquer'd but proudest of foes.
He smil'd, but the cheek of the hero grew pale—
  Huzza! and his eyes were no longer so bright;
His soul on the pinions of glory set sail,
  And Victory bore him aloft in our sight.

Our Sailors and Our Ships.

How, dashingly in sun and light, the frigate makes her way,
Her white wings spreading full and bright, beneath the glancing ray!
The gale may wake, but she will take whatever wind may come,
Fit car to bear the ocean-god upon his crystal home!

She cleaves the tide with might and pride, like war-horse freed from rein,
She treats the wave like abject slave—the Empress of the Main!
All, all shall mark the gallant bark, their hearts upon their lips,
And cry, "Columbia, who shall match thy sailors and thy ships?"

Stout forms, strong arms, and dauntless spirits dwell upon the deck,
True to their cause in calm or storm, in battle, or in wreck;
No foe will meet a coward hand, faint heart, or quailing eye;
They only know to fall or stand, to live the brave, or die!

The flag that carries round the world the stars and stripes of fame,
Must never shield a dastard knave, or strike in craven shame;
Let triumph scan her blazing page, no record shall eclipse
The glory of United States—her sailors and her ships!

The tempest's breath sweeps o'er the sea with howlings of despair,
Death walks upon the waters, but the tar must face and bear;
The bullets hiss, the broadsides pour, 'mid sulphur, blood, and smoke,
And prove a Yankee crew and craft alike are hearts of oak!

Oh, ye who live 'mid fruit and flowers, the peaceful, safe, and free,
Yield up a prayer for those who dare the perils of the sea.
"God and our right!" these are the words e'er first upon our lips,
But next shall be, "Our country's flag, our sailors, and our ships!"

O'er the Trident of Neptune.

1817.

O'er the trident of Neptune Britannia had boasted,
  Her flag long triumphantly flew,
Her fleet undisturbed round America coasted,
  Till Hull taught the foe what our seamen could do.
    Let the trumpet of fame tell the story,
    And our tars give to honor and glory.
Hark! hark! how the cannon like thunder does rattle,
Our heroes quite cool in the uproar of battle.

See the bold *Constitution* the *Guerriere* o'ertaking
  While seas from her fury divide,
The all-conquering foe, boys, our thunder is raking,
  See her Mizzen-mast falls in the deep o'er her side;
    See her hulk now our cannon balls boring,
    The blood from her scuppers is pouring.
See! see! she's aboard, shall we yield boys, no, never,
We'll fight for our rights on the Ocean forever.

Brave Hull gives the order for boarding, but wonder!
  By the board, Main and Foremast both go,
A lee gun proclaims she submits to our thunder,
  Which drowns the vain boast of our now humble foe.
    Huzza, now the conquest proclaiming,
    Our tars see the *Guerriere* flaming;
See! see! as she burns sinks the battle's commotion,
She blows up, she scatters her hulk on the ocean.

With equal force let Britannia send out her whole navy,
  Our seamen in bondage to drag,
Our heroes will send them express to old Davy,
  Or forfeit their lives in defense of their flag.
    Let the trumpet of fame tell the story,
    And our tars give to honor and glory;
Death! death! they'll prefer, ere from honor they sever,
Then glory to Hull and our navy forever.

At a Dinner to Admiral Farragut.

(O. W. HOLMES, July 6th, 1865.)

Now smiling friends and shipmates all,
  Since half our battle's won,
A broadside for our Admiral!
  Load every crystal gun!
Stand ready till I give the word,—
  You won't have time to tire —
And when that glorious name is heard,
  Then hip! hurrah! and fire!

Bow foremost sinks the rebel craft,—
  Our eyes not sadly turn
And see the pirates huddling aft
  To drop their raft astern;
Soon o'er the sea-worm's destined prey
  The lifted wave shall close,—
So perish from the face of day
  All Freedom's banded foes!

But ah! what splendors fire the sky!
  What glories greet the morn!
The storm-tost banner streams on high
  Its heavenly hues new-born!
Its red fresh dyed in heroes' blood,
  Its peaceful white more pure,
To float unstained o'er field and flood
  While earth and seas endure!

All shapes before the driving blast
  Must glide from mortal view;
Black roll the billows of the past
  Behind the present's blue,
Fast, fast, are lessening in the light
  The names of high renown,—
Van Tromp's proud bosom fades from sight,
  And Nelson's half hull down!

Scarce one tall frigate walks the sea
  Or skirts the safer shores
Of all that bore to victory
  Our stout old commodores ;
Hull, Bainbridge, Porter,—where are they ?
  The waves their answer roll,
"Still bright in memory's sunset ray,—
  God rest each gallant soul ! "

A brighter name must dim their light
  With more than noontide ray,
The Sea-king of the " River Fight,"
  The Conqueror of the Bay,—
Now then the broadside ! cheer on cheer
  To greet him safe on shore !
Health, peace, and many a bloodless year
  To fight his battle o'er !

Our Flag is There.

(By Purser JOSEPH WATSON, U. S. N.   U. S. S. *Boston*, 1829.)

Our Flag is there !   Our Flag is there !
  We hail it with three loud huzzahs !
Our Flag is there !   Our Flag is there !
  Behold the glorious Stripes and Stars !
Stout hearts have fought for that bright flag,
  Strong hands sustain'd it mast head high,
And Oh ! to see how proud it waves,
  Brings tears of joy in ev'ry eye.

  Our Flag is there !   Our Flag is there !
    We'll hail it with three loud huzzahs !
  Our Flag is there !   Our Flag is there !
    Behold the glorious Stripes and Stars !

That flag has stood the battle's roar,
  With foemen stout, with foemen brave ;
Strong hands have strove that flag to low r,
  And found a speedy wat'ry grave !
That flag is known on ev'ry shore,
  The standard of a gallant band,
Alike unstain'd in peace or war,
  It floats o'er Freedom's happy land.

    Our Flag, &c.

The Ship of State.

(H. W. LONGFELLOW.)

Sail on, sail on, thou ship of state,
  Sail on, O Union, strong and great,
Humanity, with all its fears,
  Is hanging breathless on thy fate.
We know what master laid thy keel,
  What workman wrought thy ribs of steel,
Who made each mast, each sail, each rope ;
  What anvils rang, what hammers beat ;
In what a forge, in what a heat,
  Were shaped these anchors of thy hope.

Fear not each sudden sound and shock,
  'Tis of the wave, and not the rock ;
'Tis but the flapping of the sail,
  And not a rent made by the gale.
In spite of rock, and tempest's roar,
  In spite of false lights on the shore,
Sail on, nor fear to breast the sea,
  Our hearts, our hopes, our prayers, our tears,
Our faith, triumphant o'er our fears,
  Are all with thee, are all with thee.

The Flag of Our Union.

(GEO. P. MORRIS.)

"A song for our banner," the watchword recall,
  Which gave the Republic her station ;
"United we stand, divided we fall!"
  It made and preserves us a nation !

    The union of lakes, the union of lands—
      The union of States none can sever,
    The union of hearts, the union of hands—
      And the Flag of our Union for ever and ever,
    The Flag of our Union forever !

What God in His wisdom and mercy designed,
  And armed with His weapons of thunder,
Not all the earth's despots and factions combined,
  Have the power to conquer or sunder !

    The union of lakes, &c.

The Cumberland.

(H. W. LONGFELLOW. March 8th, 1862.)

At anchor in Hampton Roads we lay,
  On board of the *Cumberland*, sloop-of-war ;
And at times from the fortress across the bay
    The alarum of drums swept past,
    Or a bugle blast
  From the camp on the shore.

Then far away to the south uprose
  A little feather of snow-white smoke,
And we knew that the iron ship of our foes
    Was steadily steering its course
    To try the force
  Of our ribs of oak.

Down upon us heavily runs,
  Silent and sullen, the floating fort ;
Then comes a puff of smoke from her guns,
  And leaps the terrible death,
    With fiery breath,
  From each open port.

We are not idle, but send her straight
  Defiance back in a full broadside !
As hail rebounds from a roof of slate,
    Rebounds our heavier hail
    From each iron scale
  Of the monster's hide.

" Strike your flag ! " the rebel cries,
  In his arrogant old plantation strain.
" Never ! " our gallant Morris replies :
    " It is better to sink than to yield ! "
    And the whole air pealed
  With the cheers of our men.

Then, like a kraken huge and black,
  She crushed our ribs in her iron grasp !
Down went the *Cumberland* all a wrack,
    With a sudden shudder of death,
    And the cannon's breath
  For her dying gasp.

Next morn, as the sun rose over the bay,
  Still floated our flag at the mainmast-head.
Lord, how beautiful was Thy day !
    Every waft of the air
    Was a whisper of prayer,
  Or a dirge for the dead.

Ho ! brave hearts that went down in the seas !
  Ye are at peace in the troubled stream.
Ho ! brave land ! with hearts like these,
    Thy flag, that is rent in twain,
    Shall be one again,
  And without a seam !

Columbia Rules the Sea.

(Music by HENRY TUCKER. Words by J. D. CANNING.)

The pennon flutters in the breeze, the anchor comes apeak ;
Let fall sheet home, the briny foam, and ocean's waste we seek ;
  The booming gun speaks our adieu, fast fades our native shore,

      Columbia free shall rule the sea,
        Britannia ruled of yore ;
      Columbia free shall rule the sea,
        Columbia evermore.

We go the tempest's wrath to dare, the billows' maddened play ;
Now climbing high against the sky, now rolling far away ;
  While Yankee oak bears Yankee hearts, courageous to the core,

      Columbia free, &c.

We'll bear her flag around the world in thunder and in flame ;
The seagirt isles a wreath of smiles shall form around her name ;
  The winds shall pipe their pæans loud, the billowy chorus roar,

      Columbia free, &c.

Ye Seamen of Columbia.

1813.

    Ye seamen of Columbia,
      Who guard your country's rights,
    Whose deeds deserve eternal fame,
      In five successive fights ;
    Oh, try your matchless skill again,
      Subdue your ancient foe,
    As they roar on your shore,
      Where the stormy tempests blow.

The spirits of ten thousand men,
   Who groan beneath the yoke,
Shall join to aid your labors,
   When you their chains have broke ;
Nor shall they e'er be press'd again,
   To serve your ancient foe,
As they roar on your shore,
   Where the stormy tempests blow.

Columbia needs no bulwarks
   Along the stormy coast,
Her gallant seamen are her walls,
   The country's pride and boast ;
There's Hull, Decatur, Porter, Jones,
   And a long list besides,
Who will sweep o'er the deep,
   And in fearless triumph ride.

The haughty flag of England
   That waved a thousand years,
Is stript of its proud laurels,
   Which on our flag appears ;
Our tars have crowned the eagle,
   And the stripes have lashed the foe,
As they sweep o'er the deep,
   Where the stormy tempests blow.

Sea and Land Victories.

From the " Naval Songster," being a collection of Naval Victories and other excellent songs.

(Printed by T. WHITS, Charlestown, 1815.)

With half the Western world at stake,
See Perry on the midland lake,
   The unequal combat dare ;
Unawed by vastly stronger pow'rs,
   He met the foe and made him ours,
   And closed the savage war,
   And closed the savage war.

Macdonough, too, on Lake Champlain,
In ships outnumbered, guns and men,
   Saw dangers thick increase ;
His trust in God and virtue's cause,
He conquer'd in the lion's jaws,
   And led the way to peace,
   And led the way to peace.

To sing each valiant hero's name
Whose deeds have swelled the files of fame,
   Requires immortal powers ;
Columbia's warriors never yield
To equal force by sea or field,
   Her Eagle never cowers.

Long as Niagara's cataract roars,
Or Erie laves our Northern shores,
   Great Brown, thy fame shall rise ;
Outnumber'd by a veteran host
Of conquering heroes, Britain's boast—
   Conquest was there thy prize.

At Plattsburg, see the Spartan band,
Where gallant Macomb held command,
   The unequal host oppose ;
Provost confounded, vanquished flies,
Convinced that numbers won't suffice
   Where Freemen are the foes.

Our songs to noblest strains we'll raise
While we attempt thy matchless praise,
   Carolina's god-like son ;
While Mississippi rolls his flood,
Or Freemen's hearts move patriot's blood,
   The palm shall be thine own.

At Orleans—lo! a savage band,
In countless numbers gain the strand,
  "Beauty and spoil" the word—
There Jackson with his fearless few,
The invincibles by thousands slew,
  And dire destruction poured.

O Britain! when the tale is told
Of Jackson's deeds by fame enrolled,
  Should grief and madness rise,
Remember God, the avenger, reigns,
Who witnessed Havre's smoking plains,
  And Hampton's female cries.

Comrades! Join the Flag of Glory.

1813.

[Tune: "Banish Sorrow."]

Comrades! join the flag of glory,
  Cheerily tread the deck of fame,
Earn a place in future story,
  Seek and win a warrior's name.

Yankee tars can laugh at danger,
  While the roaring mountain wave
Teems with carnage—they are strangers
  To a deed that is not brave.

May our bannered stars as ever
  Splendidly o'er freemen burn,
Till the night of war is over,
  Till the dawn of peace return.

The Yankee Man-of-War.

Description of the daring bravery of Captain JOHN PAUL JONES, in his cruise in the Irish Channel in 1778.

(The Ranger.)

'Tis of a gallant Yankee ship that flew the stripes and stars,
And the whistling wind from the west nor'west blew through the pitch-pine spars,
With her starboard tacks aboard, my boys, she hung upon the gale ;
On an autumn night we raised the light on the old Head of Kinsale.

It was a clear and cloudless night, and the wind blew steady and strong,
As gaily over the sparkling deep our good ship bowled along ;
With the foaming seas beneath her bow the fiery waves she spread,
And bending low her bosom of snow, she buried her lee cathead.

There was no talk of short'ning sail by him who walked the poop,
And under the press of her pond'ring jib the boom bent like a hoop!
And the groaning waterways told the strain that held her stout maintack,
But he only laughed as he glanced abaft at a white and silvery track.

The mid-tide meets in the channel waves that flow from shore to shore,
And the mist hung heavy upon the land from Featherstone to Dunmore,
And that sterling light in Tusker Rock where the old bell tolls each hour,
And the beacon light that shone so bright was quench'd on Waterford tower.

The nightly robes our good ship wore were her whole topsails three,
Her spanker and her standing jib—the courses being free,
" Now, lay aloft ! my heroes bold, not a moment must be pass'd ! "
And royals and top-gallant sails were quickly on each mast.

What looms upon our starboard bow? What hangs upon the breeze?
'Tis time our good ship hauled her wind abreast the old Saltee's,
For by her ponderous press of sail and by her consorts four
We saw our morning visitor was a British man-of-war.

Up spake our noble Captain, then, as a shot ahead of us past—
"Haul snug your flowing courses! lay your topsail to the mast!"
Those Englishmen gave three loud hurrahs from the deck of their covered ark,
And we answered back by a solid broadside from the decks of our patriot bark.

"Out booms! out booms!" our skipper cried, "out booms and give her sheet,"
And the swiftest keel that was ever launched shot ahead of the British fleet,
And amidst a thundering shower of shot with stun'sails hoisting away,
Down the North Channel Paul Jones did steer just at the break of day.

America, Commerce, and Freedom.

1815.

(From the "Boston Musical Miscellany.")

How blest the life the sailor leads,
  From clime to clime still ranging,
And as the calm the storm succeeds,
  The scene delights by changing.
When tempests howl along the main,
  Some object will remind us,

And cheer with hopes to see again
    The friends we left behind us.
Then under snug sail we laugh at the gale,
    And tho' landsmen look pale, never heed 'em,
But toss off a glass to a favorite lass,
    To America, Commerce, and Freedom,
    To America, Commerce, and Freedom.

And when arrived in sight of land,
    Or safe in port rejoicing,
Our ship we moor, our sails we hand,
    Whilst out the boat is hoisting.
With eager haste the shore we reach,
    Our friends, delighted, greet us,
And tripping lightly o'er the beach,
    The pretty lasses meet us
When the full flowing bowl has enliven'd the soul,
    To foot it we merrily lead 'em,
And each bonny lass will drink off a glass,
    To America, Commerce, and Freedom,
    To America, Commerce, and Freedom.

Our cargo sold, the chink we share,
    And gladly we receive it,
And if we meet a brother tar
    Who wants, we freely give it.
No freeborn sailor yet had store,
    But cheerfully would lend it,
And when 'tis gone, to sea for more,
    We earn it but to spend it.
Then drink round, my boys, 'tis the first of our joys,
    To relieve the distressed, clothe and feed 'em,
'Tis a task that we share with the brave and the fair,
    In this glorious land of Commerce and Freedom,
    In this glorious land of Commerce and Freedom.

On the Briny Ocean, O!

(GEORGE E. BELKNAP, U. S. N., Brookline, Mass., February 6th, 1898.)

[Air: "Wearing of the Green."]

Oh blest champagne, best Monopole,
  To Farragut we bring;
Stay not its flow, your beakers fill,
  All hail our Ocean King!
He's bunking now 'yond shot and shell
  That rained so much of woe,
He's smiling as he thinks of us
  On briny ocean, O!

CHORUS.

On briny ocean, O!
On briny ocean, O!
He's smiling as he thinks of us
On briny ocean, O!

Your glasses shift,—brim, brim with port
  Of richest purpling light;
Or red-like flame that blazed that day
  At Morgan's matchless fight.
He's resting now—that Sea King grim,
  Yet eager looks alow;
He's seeking how he'll billet us
  With Jones the peerless, O!

CHORUS—With Jones the peerless, O! &c.

To chieftain grand, our Sailor King,
  Your glasses clink again;
His River fights and Mobile Bay
  His glories aye proclaim.
He's clinging now to God's high mast,
  But fondly looks below;
He's longing now to bring-us-to
  In Viking's haven, O!

CHORUS—In Viking's haven, O! &c.

Come, hearties, come, another pull,
    Intrepid Porter sing;
How roared his guns at Fisher's fight,
    How Fisher's guns did ring!
He's breasting now Death's surging deeps,
    Afar from battle's glow;
And watching how to make us right
    With stout John Barry, O!

CHORUS—With stout John Barry, O! &c.

Now once again, your glasses fill,
    To Rowan sure and strong;
He never turned his back to foe,
    But led the fight along;
He's anchored now, in God's last port,
    Where all in time must row;
He's standing by to ration us,
    With Charlie Stewart, O!

CHORUS—With Charlie Stewart, O! &c.

Fill, fill once more, Oh, fill to brim,
    John Rodgers is our theme:
No stauncher soul e'er sailed the sea
    Nor filled Old Neptune's dream.
He's veered his chain to bitter end
    And bids our stoppers know,
If that last port, with him would make,
    With Billy Bainbridge, O!

CHORUS—With Billy Bainbridge, O! &c.

Oh, say not yet the wine is out,
    For rare DuPont we toast;
Chivalric fighter, seaman grand,
    His circling fight we boast
He's looking while we quaff to him,
    And lists our hipping, ho!
As up aloft, he lays our course
    With Hull the burly, O!

CHORUS—With Hull the burly, O! &c.

  Fresh glasses take, run Adam's ale—
   Grand Foote our tribute pay ;
  The Viking of Fort Donelson
   Best liked cold water's way.
  Now snugly moored, his hawse all clear,
   He waits the pious glow,
  The angel's trump that bids us come
   With Hazard Perry, O !

CHORUS—With Hazard Perry, O ! &c.

  Shift back your cups, spare not the wine,
   Brave Winslow's valor sound ;
  To victor of destroying chief
   Your plaudits ring around.
  He's cruising now in spirit land—
   His fame will ever grow,
  While holding fast Jim Thornton's hand
   With Tom Macdonough, O !

CHORUS—With Tom Macdonough, O ! &c.

  New bottle bring, quick, draw the cork,
   Undaunted Rhind we pledge ;
  Stout hero of the *Keokuk*
   Was never known to hedge.
  He's thinking now of powder boat
   When powder burned so slow—
  He's chumming now with bluff old Ben
   And Edward Preble, O !

CHORUS—And Edward Preble, O ! &c.

  To Worden now, best vintage pour,
   Oh, list his guns again !
  His lustrous deed on Hampton's tide
   Still stirs the world amain.
  He's sleeping now the sleep of brave,
   The sleep all heroes know ;
  He's dreaming how to station us
   With Tunis Craven, O !

CHORUS—With Tunis Craven, O ! &c.

Oh, friend and foe, must sleep alike,
   Death's angel waits us all;
His searching note with solemn sound
   Bespeaks his darkening pall.
He's beckoning now, Oh, shipmates dear,
   Stand ready, steady so;
He's minding how he'll shackle us
   At final moorings O!

CHORUS—At final moorings, O! &c.

The Freedom of the Seas.
1813.

[Tune: "Ye Gentlemen of England."]

Ye sons of free Columbia,
   Whose fathers dared the waves,
The battle and the wilderness
   To shun the fate of slaves;
The rights they bled for, and maintain
   Where'er a wave can flow,
And be free on the sea
   In despite of ev'ry foe.

CHORUS.
Though tyrants frown and cannon roar
   And the angry tempests blow!
We'll be free on the sea
   In despite of ev'ry foe.

High o'er her misty mountain tops
   Columbia's eagle soars,
And sees two mighty oceans roll
   Their tribute to her shores.
The Atlantic and the Pacific wave
   For us alike shall flow,
And we'll be free of the sea
   In despite of ev'ry foe.

   Though tyrants frown, &c.

Columbus, first of mariners,
  To us bequeathed his name,
The ocean's first great conqueror
  Resigned to us his claim.
From East to West, and round the globe,
  Where'er a wave can flow—
We'll be free on the sea
  In despite of ev'ry foe.

    Though tyrants frown, &c.

Our sires were Britons, and 'tis Heaven's
  Immutable decree,
That sons of Britons ne'er shall yield
  The freedom of the sea.
Our home, as theirs, is on the wave,
  And where a wave can flow—
We'll be free on the sea
  In despite of ev'ry foe.

    Though tyrants frown, &c.

Spread wide your arms, ye sturdy oaks,
  Ye lofty pines, ascend!
Hark!—from your hills our Navy calls
  Your towering tops to bend!
Now spread the canvas to the gale
  And where a wave can flow,
We'll be free on the sea
  In despite of ev'ry foe.

    Though tyrant's frown, &c.

Columbia's eagle flag shall fly
  All fearless o'er the flood,
To every friendly name, a dove—
  To foes, a bird of blood.
We'll bear the blessings of our land
  Where'er a wave can flow,
And be free of the sea
  In despite of ev'ry foe.

    Though tyrants frown, &c.

The Flag of the Constellation.

(Words by T. BUCHANAN REID, Florence, Italy, May, 1861.)

[Air: "Sparkling and Bright."]

The stars of our morn on our banner borne
  With the iris of heav'n are blended,
The hands of our sires first mingled those fires,
  By us they shall be defended!

CHORUS.

  Then hail the true—the Red, White, and Blue,
    The flag of the *Constellation*,
  It sails as it sailed, by our forefathers hailed,
    O'er battles that made us a nation.

What hand so bold to strike from its fold
  One star or stripe of its brightning;
To him be each star a fiery Mars,
  Each stripe a terrible lightning.

    Then hail the true, &c.

Its meteor form shall ride the storm
  Till the fiercest of foes surrender;
The storm gone by, it shall gild the sky,
  As a rainbow of peace and of splendor.

    Then hail the true, &c.

Peace, peace to the world—is our motto unfurled,
  Tho' we shun not a field that is gory;
At home or abroad, fearing none but our God,
  We will curve our own pathway to glory!

    Then hail the true, &c.

Truxton's Victory.

[Tune: "Heart of Oak."]

When Freedom, fair Freedom, her banner display'd,
Defying each foe whom her rights would invade,
Columbia's brave sons swore those rights to maintain,
And o'er ocean and earth to establish her reign.
 United they cry,
 While that standard shall fly,
 Resolved, firm, and steady,
 We always are ready
 To fight, and to conquer, to conquer or die.

Tho' Gallia through Europe has rushed like a flood,
And deluged the earth with an ocean of blood :
While by faction she's led, while she's governed by knaves,
We court not her smiles, and will ne'er be her slaves ;
 Her threats we defy,
 While our standard shall fly,
 Resolved, firm, and steady,
 We always are ready
 To fight, and to conquer, to conquer or die.

Tho' France with caprice dares our Statesmen upbraid,
A tribute demands, or sets bounds to our trade ;
From our young rising Navy our thunders shall roar,
And our Commerce extend to the earth's utmost shore.
 Our cannon we'll ply,
 While our standard shall fly ;
 Resolv'd, firm, and steady,
 We always are ready
 To fight, and to conquer, to conquer or die.

To know we're resolv'd, let them think on the hour
When Truxton, brave Truxton, off Nevis' shore,
His ship mann'd for battle, the standard unfurl'd,
And at the *Insurgente* defiance he hurl'd ;
 And his valiant tars cry,
 While our standard shall fly,
 Resolv'd, firm, and steady,
 We always are ready
 To fight, and to conquer, to conquer or die.

Each heart beat exulting, inspir'd by the cause ;
They fought for their country, their freedom and laws ;
From their cannon loud volleys of vengeance they pour'd,
And the standard of France to Columbia was lower'd.
    Huzza ! they now cry,
    Let the Eagle wave high ;
    Resolv'd, firm, and steady,
    We always are ready
    To fight, and to conquer, to conquer or die.

Then raise high the strain, pay the tribute that's due
To the fair *Constellation*, and all her brave Crew ;
Be Truxton rever'd, and his name be enroll'd,
'Mongst the chiefs of the ocean, the heroes of old.
    Each invader defy,
    While such heroes are nigh,
    Who always are ready,
    Resolv'd, firm, and steady
    To fight, and to conquer, to conquer or die.

On Board the Cumberland.

(GEO. H. BOKER, March 7th, 1862.)

"Stand to your guns, men !" Morris cried.
  Small need to pass the word ;
Our men at quarters ranged themselves
  Before the drum was heard.

And then began the sailors' jests :
  "What thing is that, I say ?"
"A long-shore meeting house adrift,
  Is standing down the bay !"

A frown came over Morris' face ;
  The strange, dark craft he knew :
"That is the iron *Merrimac*,
  Manned by a rebel crew."

"So shot your guns, and point them straight ;
  Before this day goes by,
We'll try of what her metal's made."
  A cheer was our reply.

"Remember, boys, this flag of ours
  Has seldom left its place :
And where it falls, the deck it strikes
  Is covered with disgrace."

"I ask but this : or sink or swim,
  Or live, or nobly die,
My last sight upon earth may be
  To see the Ensign fly !"

Meanwhile the shapeless, iron mass
  Came moving o'er the wave,
As gloomy as a passing hearse ;
  As silent as the grave.

Her ports were closed ; from stem to stern
  No sign of life appeared.
We wondered, questioned, strained our eyes,
  Joked—everything but feared.

She reached our range. Our broadside rang,
  Our heavy pivots roared ;
And shot and shell, a fire of hell,
  Against her sides we poured.

God's mercy ! from her sloping roof
  The iron tempest glanced,
As hail bounds from a cottage thatch,
  And round her leaped and danced.

Or when against her dusky hull
  We struck a fair, full blow,
The mighty, solid iron globes
  Were crumbled up like snow.

On, on, with fast increasing speed,
    The silent monster came ;
Though all our starboard battery
    Was one long line of flame.

She heeded not, no gun she fired,
    Straight on our bow she bore ;
Through riving plank and crashing frame
    Her furious way she tore.

Alas ! our beautiful, keen bow,
    That in the fiercest blast
So gently folded back the seas,
    They hardly felt we passed !

Alas ! alas ! my *Cumberland*,
    That ne'er knew grief before,
To be so gored, to feel so deep
    The tusk of that sea-boar !

Once more she backward drew a space,
    Once more our side she rent ;
Then, in the wantonness of hate,
    Her broadside through us sent.

The dead and dying round us lay,
    But our foemen lay abeam ;
Her open port holes maddened us ;
    We fired with shout and scream.

We felt our vessel settling fast,
    We knew our time was brief.
"Ho, man the pumps!" but they who worked,
    And fought not, wept with grief.

" Oh ! keep us but an hour afloat !
    Oh ! give us only time
To mete upon the traitors' heads
    The measure of their crime ! "

From Captain down to powder-boy
    No idle hand was then;
Two soldiers, but by chance on board,
    Fought on like sailor-men.

And when a gun's crew lost a hand,
    Some bold marine stepped out
And jerked his braided jacket off,
    And hauled the gun about.

Our forward magazine was drowned;
    And up from the sick-bay
Crawled out the wounded, red with blood,
    And round us gasping lay.

Yes, cheering, calling us by name,
    Struggling with failing breath
To keep their shipmates at their posts,
    Where Glory strove with Death.

With decks afloat, and powder gone,
    The last broadside we gave
From the gun's heated iron lips
    Burst out beneath the wave.

So sponges, rammers, and hand-spike—
    As men-of-war's-men should—
We placed within their proper racks,
    And at our quarters stood.

"Up to the spar-deck! Save yourselves!"
    Cried Selfridge. "Up, my men!
God grant that some of us may live
    To fight you ship again!"

We turned—we did not like to go:
    Yet staying seemed in vain,
Knee-deep in water; so we left,
    Some swore, some groaned with pain.

We reached the deck—there Randall stood :
  "Another turn, men—so !"
Calmly he aimed his pivot gun :
  "Now, Tenny, let her go !"

It did our sore hearts good to hear
  The song our pivot sang,
As rushing on from wave to wave
  The whirring bombshell sprang.

Brave Randall leaped upon the gun,
  And waved his cap in sport ;
"Well done ! Well aimed ! I saw that shell
  Go through an open port."

It was our last, our deadliest shot ;
  The deck was overflown :
The poor ship staggered, lurched to port,
  And gave a living groan.

Down, down, as headlong through the waves
  Our gallant vessel rushed,
A thousand gurgling watery sounds
  Around my senses gushed.

Then I remember little more,
  One look to heaven I gave,
Where, like an angel's wing I saw
  Our spotless ensign wave.

I tried to cheer, I cannot say
  Whether I swam or sank :
A blue mist closed around my eyes,
  And everything was blank.

When I awoke, a soldier lad,
  All dripping from the sea,
With two great tears upon his cheeks,
  Was bending over me.

I tried to speak ; he understood
  The wish I could not speak.
He turned to me. There, thank God ! the flag
  Still fluttered from the peak.

And there, while thread shall hang to thread,
  Oh ! let that ensign fly !
The noblest constellation set
  Against our Northern sky.

A sign that we who live may claim
  The peerage of the brave :
A monument, that needs no scroll,
  For those beneath the wave.

The Hornet; or Victory No. 5.

The Engagement took place near the mouth of the Demarara River, February 24th, 1813. In fifteen minutes the sloop-of-war *Peacock* (18), Captain PEAKE, was captured by the *Hornet* (18), Captain LAWRENCE. The *Peacock* was outmanœuvred and badly damaged in the encounter. Loss of the *Peacock*, 4 killed, including the Captain, and 33 wounded. The *Hornet* had one man killed and 2 wounded. The *Peacock* sank in five and a half fathoms of water.

1813.

[Tune : "Battle of the Nile."]

Rejoice ! rejoice ! Fredonia's sons rejoice,
  And swell the loud trumpet in patriotic strain ;
Your choice, your choice, fair freedom is your choice,
  Then celebrate her triumphs on the main ;
For the Trident of Neptune, long by Britain wielded,
At length to Fredonia reluctantly is yielded.
Then for Hull, Decatur, Jones,
And for Bainbridge, swell the tones,
While the ready hand of fame
Bright emblazons ev'ry name :
Brave Lawrence, gallant Lawrence, now is shouting with
  acclaim :

Huzza! Huzza! Huzza! Huzza! Huzza! boys,
  Free is our soil and the ocean shall be free,
Our Tars shall Mars protect beneath our stars,
  And Fredonia's Eagle hover o'er the sea.

Attend! attend! ye gallant tars attend!
  While your deeds are recounted in patriotic song;
Ascend! ascend! your banners high ascend,
  And your cannon the loud chorus still prolong.
First the bold *Constitution* led the path of glory,
The gallant little *Wasp* then added to the story,
And a brighter glory waits
The renown'd *United States*,
For she gave Columbia's fleet
The new frigate that she beat,
While the fam'd *Constitution* sank another in the deep.
    Huzza! Huzza! &c.

Again! again! Columbia's flag again
  Triumphantly floats where Britannia's used to soar,
In vain the main has own'd the *Peacock's* reign,
  Her gaudy rainbow honors are no more.
She by Lawrence, the *Hornet*, was so neatly basted,
A better roasted bird Johnny Bull never tasted;
Till she ended her career,
Like the *Java* and *Guerriere;*
For the *Hornet's* sting was ply'd
Till the sea, with blushes dy'd,
Its tyrant's fifth defeat in its bosom sought to hide.
    Huzza! Huzza! &c.

Unite! unite! Columbia's sons unite,
  And hurl on th' aggressors the tempest they provoke,
The fight is right, then raise your sabres bright,
  And Britain soon shall tremble at the stroke.
The foe is on our coast! put your mountain-oaks in motion,
Fly to the main for our wrongs are on the ocean.
There is a flood of fire,
Ev'ry tar shall breathe his ire;
His motto, while he fights,
Be, "Free Trade and Sailors' Rights,"
Till even-handed justice ev'ry injury requites.
    Huzza! Huzza! &c.

The United States and Macedonian.

1813.

How glows each patriot bosom that boasts a Yankee heart,
To emulate such glorious deeds and nobly take a part ;
    When sailors with their thund'ring guns,
    Prove to the English, French, and Dons
    That Neptune's chosen fav'rite sons
        Are brave Yankee boys.

The twenty-fifth of October, that glorious happy day,
When we, beyond all precedent, from Britons bore the sway,—
    'Twas in the ship *United States*,
    Four-and-forty guns the rates,
    That she should rule, decreed the Fates,
        And brave Yankee boys.

Decatur and his hardy tars were cruising on the deep,
When off the Western Islands they to and fro did sweep,
    The *Macedonian* they espied.
    " Huzza ! bravo ! " Decatur cried,
    " We'll humble Britain's boasted pride,
        My brave Yankee boys."

The decks were cleared, the hammocks stowed, the Boatswain pipes all hands,
The tomkins out, the guns well sponged, the Captain now commands ;
    The boys who for their country fight,
    Their words, " Free Trade and Sailors' Rights ! "
    Three times they cheered with all their might,
        Those brave Yankee boys.

Now chain-shot, grape, and langrage pierce through her oaken sides,
And many a gallant sailor's blood runs purpling in the tides ;
    While death flew nimbly o'er their decks,
    Some lost their legs, and some their necks,
    And Glory's wreath our ship bedecks,
        For brave Yankee boys.

My boys, the proud St. George's Cross, the Stripes above it wave,
And busy are our gen'rous tars, the conquered foe to save,
    Our Captain cries, "Give me your hand,"
    Then of the ship who took command
      But brave Yankee boys?

Our enemy lost her mizzen, her main and fore-top mast,
For ev'ry shot with death was winged, which slew her men so fast
    That they lost five to one in killed,
    And ten to one their blood was spilled,
    So Fate decreed and Heaven had willed,
      For brave Yankee boys.

Then homeward steered the captive ship, now safe in port she lies,
The old and young with rapture viewed our sailors' noble prize;
    Through seas of wine their health we'll drink,
    And wish them sweethearts, friends, and chink,
    Who, 'fore they'd strike, will nobly sink—
      Our brave Yankee boys.

Yankee Thunders.

1813.

[Tune: "Ye Gentlemen of England."]

Britannia's gallant streamers
  Float proudly o'er the tide,
And fairly wave Columbia's stripes,
  In battle side by side.
And ne'er did bolder seamen meet,
  Where ocean's surges pour;
O'er the tide, now they ride,
  While the bell'wing thunders roar,
While the cannon's fire is flashing fast,
  And the bell'wing thunders roar.

Chorus.

While the bell'wing thunders roar,
  While the bell'wing thunders roar,
While the cannon's fire is flashing fast,
  And the bell'wing thunders roar.

When Yankee meets the Briton
  Whose blood congenial flows,
By Heaven created to be friends,
  By fortune rendered foes ;
Hard then must be the battle fray,
  Ere well the fight is o'er ;
Now they ride, side by side,
  While the bell'wing thunders roar,
While the cannon's fire is flashing fast,
  And the bell'wing thunders roar.

    While the bell'wing thunders roar, &c.

Still, still for noble England
  Bold D'Acres' streamers fly ;
And for Columbia, gallant Hull's
  As proudly and as high ;
Now louder rings the battle's din,
  And thick the volumes pour ;
Still they ride, side by side,
  While the bell'wing thunders roar,
While the cannon's fire is flashing fast,
  And the bell'wing thunders roar.

    While the bell'wing thunders roar, &c.

Why lulls Britannia's thunder,
  That waked the watery war?
Why stays the gallant *Guerriere*
  Whose streamers waved so fair?
That streamer drinks the ocean wave,
  That warrior's fight is o'er !
Still they ride, side by side,
  While the bell'wing thunders roar,
While the cannon's fire is flashing fast,
  And the bell'wing thunders roar.

    While the bell'wing thunders roar, &c.

Hark! 'tis the Briton's lee gun!
  Ne'er bolder warrior kneeled!
And ne'er to gallant mariners
  Did braver seamen yield.
Proud be the sires, whose hardy boys
  Then fell, to fight no more:
With the brave, 'mid the wave;
  When the cannon's thunders roar,
Their spirits then shall trim the blast,
  And swell the thunder's roar.

    While the bell'wing thunders roar, &c.

Vain were the cheers of Britons,
  Their hearts did vainly swell,
Where virtue, skill, and bravery,
  With gallant MORRIS fell.
That heart so well in battle tried,
  Along the Moorish shore,
And again o'er the main,
  When Columbia's thunders roar,
Shall prove its Yankee spirit true,
  When Columbia's thunders roar.

    While the bell'wing thunders roar, &c.

Hence be our floating bulwarks
  Those oaks our mountains yield;
'Tis mighty Heaven's plain decree—
  Then take the wat'ry field!
To ocean's farthest barrier then
  Your whit'ning sail shall pour;
Safe they'll ride o'er the tide,
  While Columbia's thunders roar,
While her cannon's fire is flashing fast,
  And her Yankee thunders roar.

    While the bell'wing thunders roar, &c.

Yankee Chronology.

(Words by WILLIAM DUNLAP, 1813.)

I'll begin my chronology just at those times, sirs,
   When Britain with her thunder shook the sea and the land,
And declared truth and honor were the basest of crimes, sirs,
   And threaten'd chastisement from her mighty hand ;
But the first time she tried it, oh ! dire the disgrace, sirs,
   When Percy so bold marched to Lexington Plains,   [sirs,
But he danced "Yankee Doodle" home instead of "Chevy chase,"
   And was very glad to get back to Boston again ;

CHORUS.

   Then huzza for the sons of Columbia so free !
   They are lords of the soil, they'll be lords of the sea,
   They are lords of the soil, they'll be lords of the sea.

On the nineteenth of August in the present blessed year, sirs,
   Our brave Captain Hull met the *Guerriere* so proud,
Stout D'Acres, her commander, who had never yet known fear, sirs,
   Bade his merry men stand by and his three ensigns show'd,
But our brave *Constitution*, and our brave Yankee seamen,
   In less than forty minutes forced the Englishmen to strike,
All her masts by the board show'd our guns were served by freemen,
   And the oldest English tar swore he'd never seen the like ;

   Then huzza, &c.

Next the tight little *Wasp*, with her mettlesome sting,
   Had a mind on the ocean for a bit of a *Frolic*,
Thro' the air now the grape round, and cannister sing,
   And the British complain of a most terrible colic :
On board of the enemy soon sprung our brave seamen,
   And convinced the proud foe that 'twas vain to contend,
They found that they fought not with slaves but with freemen,
   And soon on the deck did their red cross descend ;

   Then huzza, &c.

Now Decatur, of Columbia the pride and the boast,
    In th' *United States* with a crew Washingtonian
Met a frigate of Johnny Bull's overgrown host,
    Which was christened, sure foolish enough, *Macedonian;*
The drum beat to quarters, all hands were in motion,
    Each tar bravely swore to stand fast by his gun,
And soon this unconquerable ship on the ocean,
    Was conquer'd by Yankees, to whom it was fun.

       Then huzza, &c.

Again let Fame's clarion tell to the world
    Of the second brave fight of the fam'd *Constitution*,
How her thunder upon the poor *Java* was hurled,
    And her marines thrown into direst confusion.
Short, short was the contest, ere Victory beaming,
    On the standard of Bainbridge did quickly alight,
No more was the Briton's proud banner high streaming,—
    He reluctantly owned we were bravest in fight.

       Then huzza, &c.

Next Lawrence, the brave, proudly brought up the rear,
    And of roasting the *Peacock* had scarcely begun it,
Ere her feathers were scattered, her crew was in fear,
    And the fight scarce commenced, ere the *Hornet* had won it.
But the hero, alas! in repose now is sleeping,
    In defense of our rights, he fell, gallant and brave;
Every true-hearted tar for his loss now is weeping,
    And the tears of his country shall e'er moisten his grave.

       Then huzza, &c.

Ye Parliament of England.

1813.

Ye parliament of England,
    You lords and commons, too,
Consider well what you're about,
    And what you're going to do ;
You're now to fight with Yankees,
    I'm sure you'll rue the day
You roused the Sons of Liberty
    In North America.

You first confined our commerce,
    And said our ships sha'n't trade ;
You next impressed our seamen,
    And used them as your slaves ;
You then insulted Rogers,
    While ploughing o'er the main,
And had not we declared war,
    You'd have done it o'er again.

You thought our frigates were but few,
    And Yankees could not fight,
Until brave Hull your *Guerriere* took,
    And banished her from your sight.
The *Wasp* then took your *Frolic*,
    We'll nothing say to that,
The *Poictiers* being of the line,
    Of course she took her back.

The next, your *Macedonian*,
    No finer ship could swim,
Decatur took her gilt-work off,
    And then he sent her in.
The *Java*, by a Yankee ship
    Was sunk, you all must know ;
The *Peacock* fine, in all her plume,
    By Lawrence down did go.

Then, next you sent your *Boxer*
   To box us all about,
But we had an *Enterprising* brig
   That beat your *Boxer* out;
We boxed her up to Portland,
   And moored her off the town,
To show the sons of liberty
   The *Boxer* of renown.

The next, upon Lake Erie,
   Where Perry had some fun,
You own he beat your naval force,
   And caused them for to run;
This was to you a sore defeat,
   The like ne'er known before—
Your British squadron beat complete—
   Some took, some run ashore.

There's Rogers, in the *President*,
   Will burn, sink, and destroy;
The *Congress*, on the Brazil coast,
   Your commerce will annoy;
The *Essex*, in the South Seas,
   Will put out all your lights,
The flag she waves at her mast-head—
   "Free Trade and Sailors' Rights."

Lament, ye sons of Britain,
   Far distant is the day,
When you'll regain by British force
   What you've lost in America;
Go tell your King and parliament,
   By all the world 'tis known,
That British force, by sea and land,
   By Yankees is o'erthrown.

·Use every endeavor,
   And strive to make a peace,
For Yankee ships are building fast,
   Their Navy to increase ;
They will enforce their commerce,
   The laws by Heaven were made,
That Yankee ships, in time of peace,
   To any port may trade.

The Constellation and the Insurgente.

1813.

On the 9th of February, 1799, Commodore Truxton, while cruising in the West Indies in the *Constellation* (36), captured the French frigate *L'Insurgente* (40), Captain Barreau, commanding, after one hour's sharp fighting, and with a loss of only 1 killed and 3 wounded. The Frenchman lost 70 in killed and wounded.

Come, all ye Yankee sailors, with swords and pikes advance,
'Tis time to try your courage and humble haughty France ;
   The sons of France our seas invade,
   Destroy our commerce and our trade,
   'Tis time the reck'ning should be paid !
      To brave Yankee boys.

On board the *Constellation*, from Baltimore we came,
We had a bold commander and Truxton was his name !
   Our ship she mounted forty guns,
   And on the main so swiftly runs,
   To prove to France Columbia's sons
      Are brave Yankee boys.

We sailed to the West Indies in order to annoy
The invaders of our commerce, to burn, sink, and destroy ;
   Our *Constellation* shone so bright,
   The Frenchmen could not bear the sight,
   And away they scamper'd in a fright
      From the brave Yankee boys.

'Twas on the 9th of February, at Montserrat we lay,
And there we spy'd the *Insurgente* just at the break of day,
    We raised the orange and the blue,
    To see if they our signals knew,
    The *Constellation* and her crew
      Of brave Yankee boys.

Then all hands were called to quarters, while we pursued in chase,
With well prim'd guns, our tompions out, well splic'd the main brace.
    Soon to the French we did draw nigh,
    Compell'd to fight, they were, or fly,
    The word was passed, "Conquer or die,"
      My brave Yankee boys.

Loud our cannons thunder'd with peals tremendous roar,
And death upon our bullets' wings that drenched their decks with [gore.
    The blood did from their scuppers run,
    The chief exclaimed, "We are undone,"
    Their flag they struck, the battle won
      By the brave Yankee boys.

Then to St. Kitts we steered, we bro't her safe in port,
The grand salute was fired and answered from the fort.
    John Adams in full bumpers toast,
    George Washington, Columbia's boast,
    And now "the girl we love the most!"
      My brave Yankee boys.

Liberty Tree.

(ROBERT TREAT PAYNE.)

    In a chariot of light, from the regions of day
      The goddess of Liberty came;
    Ten thousand celestials directed the way,
      And hither conducted the dame.
    A fair budding branch from the gardens above
      Where millions with millions agree,
    She brought in her hand as a pledge of her love,
      And the plant she called Liberty Tree.

The celestial exotic struck deep in the ground,
  Like a native it flourished and bore ;
The fame of its fruit drew the nations around,
  To seek out its peaceable shore.
Unmindful of names or distinctions they came,
  For freemen like brothers agree ;
With one spirit endued, they one friendship pursued,
  And their temple was Liberty Tree.

Beneath this fair tree, like the patriarchs of old
  Their bread in contentment they ate,—
Unvexed with the trouble of silver and gold,
  The cares of the grand and the great ;
With timber and tar they old England supplied,
  And supported her power on the sea ;
Her battles they fought without getting a groat,
  For the honor of Liberty Tree.

But hear, O ye swains ! ('tis a tale most profane,)
  How all the tyrannical powers,—
Kings, Commons, and Lords - are uniting amain
  To cut down this guardian of ours.
From the East to the West blow the trumpet to arms,
  Through the land let the sound of it flee,
Let the far and the near all unite with a cheer,
  In defense of our Liberty Tree.

God Save Our President.

(HARRISON MILLARD.)

God save our President from every harm !
  Shield and protect him with Thy mighty arm ;
Guide him in ev'ry act, Thou Lord of us all,
Send him prosperity, sustain, lest he fall !
Send him prosperity, on Thee we call,
  God save our President from every harm.

God save our President ; watch o'er his life ;
Firm may he guide us on thro' every strife ;
Rule Thou his judgment still, Thou Ruler benign !
Strengthen him evermore, with Thy strength divine,
Strengthen him evermore,—his heart be Thine ?
God save our President from every harm.

God save our President, we humbly pray !
Lord of all nations, oh, be Thou his stay !
Hear us with one acclaim, we cry unto Thee,
Keep Thou our leader true, where'er he may be ;
Keep Thou our leader true, from error free !
God save our President from every harm.
Amen.

The Banner of the Stars.

(CAPT. R. W. RAYMOND.)

Hurrah ! boys, hurrah ! fling our banner to the breeze !
Let the enemies of freedom see its folds again unfurled :
And down with the pirates that scorn upon the seas
Our victorious Yankee banner, sign of Freedom to the World !

Chorus.

We'll never have a new flag, for ours is the true flag,
The true flag, the true flag, the Red, White and Blue flag ;
Hurrah ! boys, hurrah ! we will carry to the wars
The old flag, the free flag, the Banner of the stars !

And what though its white shall be crimsoned with our blood ?
And what though its stripes shall be shredded in the storms ?
To the torn flag, the worn flag, we'll keep our promise good,
And we'll bear the starry blue field, with gallant hearts and arms.

We'll never have a new flag, &c.

Then, cursed be he who would strike our Starry Flag !
May the God of Hosts be with us, as we smite the traitor down !
And cursed be he who would hesitate or lag
Till the dear flag, the fair flag, with Victory we crown.

We'll never have a new flag, &c.

The Navy.

1813.

When Fame shall tell the splendid story,
Of COLUMBIA'S naval glory,
Since first victorious o'er the deep,
Our starry flag was seen to sweep ;
The glowing tale will form a page,
To grace the annals of the age,
And teach our sons to proudly claim
The brightest meed of naval fame.
In lofty strains the bard shall tell
How TRUXTON fought, how SOMERS fell !
How gallant PREBLE'S daring host
Triumph'd along the Moorish coast ;
Forc'd the proud infidel to treat,
And brought the Crescent to their feet !

And mark amidst the splendid band
That guards COLUMBIA'S boundless strand,
The youthful hero of the wave,
DECATUR, bravest of the brave !
And RODGERS, whose triumphant name
Sounds from the trump of future fame !
And, Oh ! forget not in the song,
That bears my country's fame along !
Victorious HULL, and conquering JONES,
COLUMBIA'S own intrepid sons !
Whose matchless skill and well-serv'd thunder,
Struck the proud flag of England under,
And threw, by hearts of Freemen brave,
The British Lion in the wave !
Masters of verse, Oh ! still proclaim,
In song sublime, their glorious fame,
Till time evolves the fated day,
That sweeps these Union States away ;
Or, verging from its sinking shore,
The rolling ocean foams no more !

And who that hears this splendid story,
This brilliant tale of naval glory,
Feels not the patriot-warmth, and fire
Of Prophecy his soul inspire?
—Lifting th' eternal veil away,
That shrouds futurity from day ;
And, after many a deed that cheers
The distant days of future years,
Reads upon every standard high,
That waves our Eagles to the sky,
(With warm delight, and proud emotion)
"COLUMBIA, *Mistress of the Ocean!*"

The Hornet and the Peacock.

1813.

Ye sons of Columbia, true lords of the main,
Exult in the pride of your prowess again ;
The flag of Old England now kisses the wave,
And the throne of her glory has proven its grave !
      Then, Freemen, rejoice,
      In a fullness of voice,
In the glorious deeds of your heroes rejoice !

'Tis an old Yankee saying of serious mood,
That's "a *plaguey* poor wind which blows nobody good ;"
But each breeze that blows o'er the wide swelling sea
Wafts the tidings of VICT'RY, Columbia, to thee.
      Then swell the glad sound,
      Let the tidings resound,
Wherever the heart of a freeman is found !

We sing how the *Peacock*, in arrogant pride,
Our snug little *Hornet* provok'd on the tide ;
But what could the power of a *Peacock* prevail ?
For a *Hornet*, you know, has a *sting* in her tail.
      Then join in the song,
      And their memories prolong,
Who're asserting our rights, and avenging each wrong,

Her *crown* being seiz'd by our Eagle's firm beak,
In the time of a twinkling she dows'd down her *Peake*,
And short was the action, tho' long live the deed
Which caus'd a new vein of proud Britain to bleed.
   And LAWRENCE, thy name,
   Through the trumpet of Fame,
 The praise of thy countrymen loud shall proclaim.

In *fifteen* short minutes!—'tis true Yankee time:
There even the horrors of death were sublime!
Let them say we're *superior*,—a matter of course;
For the *bravest*, though *least*, are superior in force!
   And down they must go,
   To the regions below,
 The fate of the *Guerriere* and *Java* to know.

And now the vain boasters of Britain may tell,
That 'tis merely by *chance* that we drub them so well;
And so let it be—but *per chance* they shall know,
That a *small* chance have *they*, when a Yankee's their foe!
   Then success to the brave,
   Who their *chance* on the wave
 Have ventur'd, the rights of their country to save!

Now Bainbridge, and Jones, and Decatur, and Hull,
And LAWRENCE, have each by the horns took John Bull—
They've stung him to *roaring*—but all in *good part*—
'Twas merely a *Frolic* of true Yankee art!
   Encore, then encore!
   Let him roar, let him roar!
 Once more, while he *can*, let him roar! let him roar!

And now to the heroes who yielded their lives,
And they who returned to their sweethearts and wives:
May those find in heaven a merited berth,
And these, while they're living, a *heaven on earth!*
   Then push round the bowl,
   In the fullness of soul,
 In the spirit of patriots, disdaining control!

Now Coil Up Your Nonsense.

1817.

Now coil up your nonsense 'bout England's great navy,
    And take in your slack about oak-hearted tars ;
For frigates as stout, and as gallant crews have we,
    Or how came her *Macedon* deck'd with our stars?
Yes—how came her *Guerriere*, her *Peacock* and *Java*,
    All sent broken ribb'd to old Davy of late?
How came it? Why, split me! than Britons we're braver,
    And that shall they feel, too, wherever we meet.

CHORUS.

    Then charge the can cheerily,
    Send it round merrily ;
Here's to our country, and captains commanding ;
    To all who inherit
    Of Lawrence the spirit,
" Disdaining to strike while a stick is left standing."

Now, if unawares, we should run (a fresh gale in)
    Close in with a squadron, we'd laugh at 'em all ;
We'd tip Master Bull such a sample of sailing,
    As should cause him to fret like a pig in a squall ;
We'd show the vain boaster of numbers superior,
    Tho' he and his slaves at the notion may sneer,
In skill, as in courage, to us they're inferior ;
    For the longer they chase us the less we've to fear,

    Then charge, &c.

But should a Razee be espied ahead nearly ;
    To fetch her we'd crowd every stitch we could make ;
Down chests and up hammocks would heave away cheerily,
    And ready for action would be in a shake :
For her swaggering cut, though, and metal not caring,
    Till up with her close should our fire be withheld ;
Then pour'd in so hot that her mangled crew, fearing
    A trip to the bottom, should speedily yield.

    Then charge, &c.

Britannia, altho' she beleaguers our coast now,
  The dread of our wives, and our sweethearts as well,
Of ruling the waves has less reason to boast now,
  As Dacres, and Carden, and Whinyates can tell :
Enroll'd in our annals live Hull and Decatur,
  Jones, Lawrence and Bainbridge, Columbia's pride,
The pride of our navy, which, sooner or later,
  Shall on the wide ocean triumphantly ride.

    Then charge, &c.

The American Sailor.

(1813.)

Ye honest tars of Yankee mould,
Whose gallant actions fame has told !
Permit a brother tar to greet
The flag of our "MOSQUITO FLEET,"
Which you have taught to triumph o'er
The flag which rul'd the waves before.

Our CONSTITUTION first began
T' assert the equal "rights of man"
In that domain where Britain's pride
Those rights to other realms denied—
But HULL soon sent her *Guerriere's* bones
To seek a berth with Davy Jones.

Our little WASP on dauntless wing,
Had flown abroad to try her sting,
And being both alert and brave,
She took a FROLIC on the wave ;
But this so far impair'd her might,
A stronger " Foeman " stopp'd her flight.

A happier victory the Fates
Decreed for the UNITED STATES—
DECATUR on that brilliant day,
Might " *veni, vidi, vici*," say :
For Briton's naval empire shook
When he the *Macedonian* took !

Again the CONSTITUTION weigh'd,
To distant realms our Stars display'd ;
Where BAINBRIDGE, fir'd by manly zeal,
Made arrogance his prowess feel ;
For there he foil'd his vaunting foe,
And laid the JAVA'S standard low !

Our ships are staunch, our tars are brave,
As ever plough'd the azure wave ;
We wish—when they abroad must roam—
To bear the peaceful Olive home—
But if insulting foes they meet,
With laurels they will load our fleet !

Superior traits of nautic skill,
Columbia's log-book oft shall fill ;
And there each gallant captain's name
This verse shall consecrate to Fame—
" From equal force he'll never fly,
But conquer, or most nobly die."

The Constitution and Guerriere.

1813.

COLUMBIA'S sons, prepare, unite,
Now for your Country's Freedom fight,
And with your swords maintain your rights,
    'Gainst pride and persecution;
And while you scourge our haughty foes,
I'll sing the martial deeds of those,
    Whose metal tried,
    Soon low'r'd the pride
Of DACRES, who brave HULL defied
    On board the CONSTITUTION.

Nineteenth of August, half-past two,
And past meridian came in view,
The *Guerriere* frigate and her crew,
    All fir'd with resolution;
The boasting chieftain bent his course,
Resolv'd to put his threats in force,
    And with his guns
    Subdue the sons
Of Yankees, who no danger shuns,
    On board the CONSTITUTION.

Our gallant ship now swiftly flies,
And ev'ry man his gun supplies,
While our commander cheerly cries,
    Evince your resolution:
With ardor each to action springs,
While with three cheers the welkin rings:
    Our foes amaz'd,
    With wonder gaz'd,
To see Columbia's Standard rais'd
    On board the CONSTITUTION.

The *Guerriere's* balls flew thick and hot
Around us, which we answer'd not,
But steer'd till within pistol shot,
    Resolv'd on execution :
Our first broadside like thunder roar'd,
And brought his mizzen by the board,
    Her mainmast too,
    And foremast flew
In pieces, while our jovial crew,
    Huzza'd for the CONSTITUTION.

When DACRES first receiv'd this check,
And found the *Guerriere* all a wreck,
Himself a pris'ner on the deck,
    His ship's crew in confusion ;
Perceiv'd the Yankee boys on board,
With grief beheld the Union low'r'd,
    All hope now fled,
    He sighing said,
The God of War to victory led
    Brave HULL in the CONSTITUTION.

The Briton oft had made his boast,
He'd with his crew, a chosen host,
Pour fell destruction 'round the coast,
    And work a revolution :
Urg'd with pride, a challenge sent
Bold RODGERS in the *President*,
    Wishing to meet
    Him tete-a-tete,
Or one his equal from our fleet,
    Such was the CONSTITUTION.

Columbia's sons, each jovial soul,
Whose glowing breast contemns control,
Rejoice around the sparkling bowl,
    While wine flows in profusion.
First MADISON, our country's boast,
The Congress next, shall be our toast,
    Our third is due
    Brave HULL and crew,
Then all who hold our rights in view,
    And guard the CONSTITUTION.

The Alarmed Skipper.

(JAMES T. FIELDS.)

"It was an ancient mariner."

Many a long, long year ago,
    Nantucket skippers had a plan
Of finding out, though "lying low,"
    How near New York their schooners ran.

They greased the lead before it fell,
    And then, by sounding through the night,
Knowing the soil that stuck, so well,
    They always guessed their reckoning right.

A skipper gray, whose eyes were dim,
    Could tell, by *tasting*, just the spot;
And so below he'd "dowse the glim,"—
    After, of course, his "something hot."

Snug in his berth, at eight o'clock,
    This ancient skipper might be found;
No matter how his craft would rock,
    He slept,—for skippers' naps are sound.

The watch on deck would now and then
    Run down and wake him, with the lead;
He'd up, and taste, and tell the men
    How many miles they went ahead.

One night, 'twas Jotham Marden's watch,
    A curious wag,— the peddler's son,
And so he mused (the wanton wretch),
    "To-night I'll have a grain of fun.

"We're all a set of stupid fools
    To think the skipper knows by *tasting*
What ground he's on,— Nantucket schools
    Don't teach such stuff, with all their *basting!*"

And so he took the well-greased lead
    And rubbed it o'er a box of earth
That stood on deck,—a parsnip bed,—
    And then he sought the skipper's berth.

"Where are we now, sir? Please to taste."
    The skipper yawned, put out his tongue,
Then oped his eyes in wondrous haste,
    And then upon the floor he sprung!

The skipper stormed, and tore his hair,
    Thrust on his boots, and roared to Marden,
"*Nantucket's sunk, and here we are
    Right over old Marm Hacket's garden!*"

How Sleep the Brave.

(WILLIAM COLLINS, 1720-1756.)

How sleep the brave who sink to rest
By all their Country's wishes blest!
When Spring, with dewy fingers cold,
Returns to deck their hallow'd mould,
She there shall dress a sweeter sod
Than fancy's feet have ever trod.

By fairy hands their knell is rung,
By forms unseen their dirge is sung:
There Honor comes, a pilgrim gray,
To bless the turf that wraps their clay,
And Freedom shall awhile repair
To dwell a weeping hermit there!

The Ballad of the Oysterman.

(OLIVER WENDELL HOLMES.)

It was a tall young oysterman lived by the river-side ;
His shop was just upon the bank, his boat was on the tide ;
The daughter of a fisherman, that was so straight and slim,
Lived over on the other bank, right opposite to him.

It was the pensive oysterman that saw a lovely maid
Upon a moonlight evening, a-sitting in the shade ;
He saw her wave her handkerchief, as much as if to say,
"I'm wide awake, young oysterman, and all the folks away."

Then up arose the oysterman, and to himself said he,
" I guess I'll leave the skiff at home, for fear that folks should see ;
I read it in the story-book, that, for to kiss his dear,
Leander swam the Hellespont,—and I will swim this here."

And he has leaped into the waves, and crossed the shining stream,
And he has clambered up the bank all in the moolight gleam ;
O, there were kisses sweet as dew, and words as soft as rain,—
But they have heard the father's step, and in he leaps again !

Out spoke the ancient fisherman,—"O, what was that my daughter?"
"'Twas nothing but a pebble, sir, I threw into the water."
"And what is that, pray tell me, love, that paddles off so fast?"
"It's nothing but a porpoise, sir, that's been a-swimming past."

Out spoke the ancient fisherman,—"Now bring me my harpoon !
I'll get into my fishing boat, and fix the fellow soon."
Down fell that pretty innocent, as falls a snow-white lamb,
Her hair drooped 'round her pallid cheeks, like sea-weed on a clam.

Alas for those two loving ones ! she waked not from her swound,
And he was taken with the cramp, and in the waves was drowned ;
But Fate has metamorphosed them, in pity of their woe,
And now they keep an oyster-shop for mermaids down below.

This Life, Boys, at Best's but a Rough Sort of Trip.

1817.

This life, boys, at best's but a rough sort of trip,
   And we've nothing but honor to lose ;
So, 'tis better, d'ye see, ere we give up the ship,
   Like Lawrence to finish life's cruise.
      For I fancy we'll all meet at Davy's again,
      As jovial as e'er we met here.

Then what do we value the scoff on the free,
   That from France and from England's self starts?
They may count us their hulks till they're tired, d'ye see,
   And we'll count them as many true hearts
      That can stick to their moorings through life's foulest squalls,
      And still face the world as it goes.

So the ninnies we'll balk who dare think we'll descend,
   Our rights on the seas to forego—
We have biscuit and grog for a true-hearted friend,
   And a merry three cheers for a foe :
      For the world and its great ones may change as they please,
      But a sailor's a sailor, boys, still.

Then let the cold heart in its own baseness freeze,
   That thinks we'll be shy on the waves—
Shall we skulk, boys, and hunt by-ways, thro' the seas
   Like cowardly rovers or slaves?
      Away with such gabble and nonsense, say I,
      While we've Yankee colors to show.

We don't know the count of his ships who's our foe,
   And, what is yet more, we don't care ;
For ourselves, to the very heart's core, lads, we know ;
   And so, come foul weather or fair,
      I'm for setting top-gallants and booming ahead,
      And we'll turn by for none as we go.

Then huzza! for free trade, and our rights as we be,
  'Tis a whim that we like more and more;
And sailors must have out their whims, d'ye see,
  Whether fighting or jigging on shore—
    So huzza! for free trade and for colors mast high,
    No skulking or quibbling for me.

Whether Bainbridge, or Hull, or Decatur commands,
  Rodgers, Biddle, or Jones, 'tis all one—
Huzza! and huzza! and huzza! sing all hands,
  And yard-arm to yard-arm's the fun!
    Then lubbers stand clear, we have work to do, boys,
    For 'tis England's old cross must come down.

And we'll rake till sly death our heart's cables shall slip,
  The command that our Lawrence has given—
He was dying—says he, "Boys, don't give up the ship!"
  And the words took his soul off to Heaven.
    Brave heart! he has gone to his rest! never mind,
    We are here to fight under him still.

So, no more of vain talking, or whining, or art—
  We've to fight for the rights of the States;
And, with Honor our pilot, and Justice our chart,
  Good humor and friendship our mates:
    They'll find, if we've biscuit and grog for a friend,
    We've a merry three cheers for a foe.

Yankee Doodle.

(Song of the Revolutionary period)

Father and I went down to camp,
  Along with Captain Gooding;
There we see the men and boys
  As thick as hasty pudding.

Chorus.

Yankee doodle, keep it up,
  Yankee doodle dandy;
Mind the music and the step,
  And with the girls be handy.

And there we see a thousand men,
    As rich as Squire David ;
And what they wasted every day
    I wish it could be saved.

    Yankee doodle, &c.

The 'lasses they eat every day
    Would keep a house a winter ;
They have so much that I'll be bound
    They eat it when they're mind to.

    Yankee doodle, &c.

And there we see a swamping gun,
    Large as a log of maple,
Upon a deuced little cart—
    A load for father's cattle.

    Yankee doodle, &c.

And every time they shoot it off
    It takes a horn of powder ;
It makes a noise like father's gun,
    Only a nation louder.

    Yankee doodle, &c.

I went as nigh to one myself
    As Siah's under-pinning ;
And father went as nigh again,
    I thought the deuce was in him.

    Yankee doodle, &c.

Cousin Simon grew so bold
    I thought he would have cock'd it ;
It scared me so, I streak'd it off,
    And hung by father's pocket.

    Yankee doodle, &c.

But Captain Davis had a gun,
  He kind of slapped his hand on't.
He struck a crooked stabbing iron
  Upon the little end on't.
    Yankee doodle, &c.

And there I see a pumpkin shell
  As big as mother's basin,
And every time they touch'd it off
  They scamper'd like the nation.
    Yankee doodle, &c,

I see a little barrel, too,
  The heads were made of leather,
They knocked upon it with little clubs,
  And called the folks together.
    Yankee doodle, &c.

And there was Captain Washington,
  And gentle folks about him ;
They say he's grown so tarnal proud
  He will not ride without 'em.
    Yankee doodle, &c.

He got him on his meeting clothes,
  Upon a strapping stallion ;
He set the world along in rows,
  In hundreds and in millions.
    Yankee doodle, &c.

The flaming ribbons in their hats,
  They looked so tearing fine, ah :
I wanted plaguily to get,
  To give to my Jemima.
    Yankee doodle, &c.

I see another snarl of men,
    A-digging graves, they told me,
So tarnal long, so tarnal deep,
    They 'tended they should hold me.

    Yankee doodle, &c,

It scared me so, I hook'd it off,
    Nor stopped, as I remember;
Nor turn'd about till I got home,
    Lock'd up in mother's chamber.

    Yankee doodle, &c.

Yankee Doodle, No. 2.

Ye gallant sons of Liberty,
    Who bravely have defended
Your country's rights by land or sea,
    And to her cause attended.

Chorus.

    Yankee Doodle is the tune
        The Americans delight in,
    It will do to whistle, sing, and play,
        And just the thing for fighting.

Upon the ocean's wide domain
    Our tars are firm and true, sirs,
And Freedom's cause they will maintain
    With Yankee doodle doo, sirs.

    Yankee doodle, &c.

The Fourth Day of July, 'tis said,
    That day did Britain rue, sirs,
When an independent tune we play'd,
    Called Yankee doodle doo, sir.

    Yankee doodle, &c.

Columbia's sons did then declare
   They would be independent,
And for King George they would not care,
   Not yet for his descendant.

   Yankee doodle, &c.

British tars think that they can
   Whip Yankees, one to two, sirs;
But only give us man to man,
   They'll see what we can do, sirs.

   Yankee doodle, &c.

Yankee doodle, boys, huzza!
   Down outside, up the middle,
Yankee doodle, fa so la,
   Trumpet, drum, and fiddle.

   Yankee doodle, &c.

Red, White, and Blue.

(DAVID T. SHAW.)

Oh, Columbia, the gem of the ocean,
   The home of the brave and the free;
The shrine of each patriot's devotion,
   A world offers homage to thee.
Thy mandates make heroes assemble,
   When liberty's form stands in view;
Thy banners make tyranny tremble,
   When borne by the red, white, and blue.

Chorus.

When borne by the red, white, and blue,
When borne by the red, white, and blue,
Thy banners make tyranny tremble,
When borne by the red, white, and blue.

When war waged its wide desolation,
    And threatened our land to deform,
The ark then of freedom's foundation,
    Columbia rode safe through the storm.
With her garland of victory o'er her,
    When so proudly she bore her bold crew,
With her flag proudly floating before her,
    The boast of the red, white, and blue.

    The boast, &c.

The wine cup, the wine cup bring hither,
    And fill you it up to the brim,
May the memory of Washington ne'er wither,
    Nor the star of his glory grow dim.
May the service united ne'er sever,
    And each to our colors prove true ;
The army and navy for ever,
    Three cheers for the red, white, and blue.

    Three cheers, &c.

Columbia! Arise to Glory!

Columbia! Columbia! to glory arise !
The Queen of the Free, and the Child of the Wise !
Thy freedom shall crown thee with splendors untold,
And thro' ages on ages thy charms shall unfold :
For thy throne is the last and the noblest of Time,
By no shame undermined, and upheld by no crime !
With the future thy dower, and its blessings thy prize,
Columbia! Columbia! to glory arise !

Thy fleets o'er all oceans thy flag shall display,
The lands shall admire, and the seas shall obey ;
Each clime for thy marts shall its tributes unfold,
And the East and the South yield their spices and gold ;
As the day-spring unbounded thy blessings shall flow,
Till on all the broad earth thou shalt freedom bestow,
And the nations in Union shall mingle their cries —
Columbia! Columbia! to glory arise !

Our Country's Our Ship.

(DIGNUM, 1800.)

Our country is our ship, d'ye see :
  A gallant vessel, too ;
And well may he a proud man be
  Who's one of her bold crew.
Each man, where'er his station be,
  When Duty's call commands,
    Should take his stand
    And lend a hand,
As the common cause demands.

And when our haughty enemies
  This noble ship assail,
Let all brave hearts despise the arts
  Wherewith they would prevail ;
And he who skulks to traitor hulks,
  Or hides in fear below,
    May shark or rope
    Soon end his hope,
And the devil no mercy show !

Among ourselves, like foolish elves,
  We oft may make a rout,
And having naught for better thought,
  Resolve to fight it out ;
But once behold our foes of old,
  Shake hands, boys ! let's be friends !
    And on the deck,
    Till all's a wreck,
Each heart the old ship defends !

A Union Ship and a Union Crew.

A Union ship and a Union Crew,
　　Tally hi ho, you know!
O, her flag is the flag of the red, white, and blue,
　　With the stars aloft and alow;
Her sails are spread for the Northern breeze,
　　And she dashes the spray from her prow,
For her flag is the proudest that floats o'er the seas,
　　And 'tis shining the loveliest now!

　　O, a Union Ship and a Union Crew, &c.

A Union Ship and a Union Crew,
　　Tally hi ho, you know!
Every man aboard is a patriot true,
　　Whether placed aloft or alow;
Though the black'ning sky and the whistling wind
　　Are foretelling a Southern gale,
Not a lubber you'll see, not a skulker you'll find,
　　For the cry is on deck there! a sail!
There are pirates astern, but we'll give them a shot—
　　To the guns aloft and alow!

　　A Union ship, &c.

My Own Native Land.

I've roamed over mountain, I've crossed over flood;
　　I've traversed the wave-rolling sand;
Tho' the fields were as green, and the moon shone as bright,
　　Yet it was not my own native land!
　　　　No, no, no, no!
　　　　It was not my own native land!

The right hand of friendship how oft have I grasped,
   And bright eyes have smiled and looked bland,
Yet happier far were the hours that I passed
   In my own, in my dear native land !
      My own native land !
        Far, far in my own native land !

Then hail, dear Columbia ! the land that we love,
   Where flourishes Liberty's tree !
'Tis the birth-place of Freedom our own native home—
   'Tis the land, 'tis the land of the Free !
      Yes, yes, yes, yes !
        'Tis the land of the Free—of the Free !

The American Star.

[Air : "Humors of Glen."]

1815.

Come, strike the bold anthem, the war-dogs are howling,
   Already they eagerly snuff up their prey ;
The red clouds of war o'er our dwellings are scowling,
   Soft Peace spreads her wings and flies weeping away ;
Our infants affrighted, cling close to their mothers,
   Our youth grasp their swords, and for combat prepare,
Whilst Beauty is weeping for husbands and brothers,
   Who march to defend the American Star !

Come, blow the shrill bugle, the wild drum awaken,
   The dread rifle seize, and let cannons loud roar,
No heart with pale fear or faint doubtings be shaken,
   No slave's hostile foot leave a print on our shore !
Shall mothers, wives, daughters, and sisters, left weeping,
   Insulted by ruffians, be dragg'd to despair !
O, no ! from her hills the proud eagle comes sweeping,
   And waves to the brave the American Star !

The spirits of Washington, Warren, Montgomery,
    Look down from the clouds with bright aspect serene!
Come, sailors! a tear and a toast to their memory!
    Rejoicing they'll see us as once they have been!
To us the high boon, by the gods has been granted,
    To speed the glad tidings of Liberty far;
Let millions invade us, we'll meet them undaunted,
    And vanquish them by the American Star!

Your hands, then, dear comrades, round Liberty's altar
    United we'll swear by the souls of the brave!
No one from the strong resolution shall falter,
    We'll live independent or sink to the grave:
Then, freemen, fill up! lo! our striped banner's flying,
    The proud bird of liberty soars through the air!
Beneath her bright pinions Oppression is dying!
    Success to the beaming American Star!

Battle Chorus.

[Air: "Suoni la Tromba."—I PURITANI.]

Hark! to the voiceful anthem
    Joining in mighty jubilation;
Lo! 'tis our Liberty's ovation
    Swelling the chorus of a world!
Proudly our country is awaking.
    Grandly is swelling now her chorus,
    Whilst, like a beacon flaming o'er us,
    Freedom's starry flag is unfurl'd!

    Hark! to the voiceful anthem. (*Repeat.*)

The American Boy.

"Father, look up and see that flag,
  How gracefully it flies;
Those pretty stripes—they seem to be
  A rainbow in the skies."

"It is your country's flag, my son,
  And proudly drinks the light;
O'er ocean's waves, in foreign climes,
  A symbol of our might."

"Father, what fearful noise is that,
  Like thundering of the clouds?
Why do the people wave their hats,
  And rush along in crowds?"

"It is the noise of cannon, boy,
  The glad shouts of the free;
This is the day to memory dear—
  'Tis Freedom's Jubilee."

"I wish that I were now a man,
  I'd fire my cannon, too,
And cheer as loudly as the rest—
  But, father, why don't you?"

"I'm getting old and weak—but still
  My heart is big with joy;
I've witnessed many a day like this—
  Shout you aloud, my boy."

"Hurrah for Freedom's Jubilee!
  God bless our native land!
And may I live to hold the sword
  Of Freedom in my hand!"

"Well done, my boy—grow up and love
The land that gave you birth;
A home where Freedom loves to dwell
Is paradise on earth."

Viva l'America.

(Lieut. H. MILLARD.)

Noble Republic! happiest of lands,
Foremost of nations Columbia stands;
Freedom's proud banner floats in the skies,
Where shouts of Liberty daily arise,
"United we stand, divided we fall,"
Union for ever—freedom to all.

CHORUS.

Throughout the world our motto shall be
Viva l'America, home of the free.

Should ever a traitor rise in the land,
Curs'd be his homestead, withered his hand;
Shame be his mem'ry, scorn be his lot,
Exile his heritage, his name a blot!
"United we stand, divided we fall,"
Granting a home and freedom to all.

CHORUS—Throughout the wide world, &c.

To all her heroes, Justice and Fame;
To all her foes, a traitor's foul name;
Our "Stripes and Stars" still proudly shall wave,
Emblem of Liberty, flag of the brave,
"United we stand, divided we fall;"
Gladly we'll die, at our country's call.

CHORUS—Throughout the wide world, &c.

Hurrah for the White, Red, and Blue.

[Air: " Bonnets o' Blue."]

Hush'd is the clamorous trumpet of war,
Hush'd, hush'd is the trumpet of war;
The soldier's retired from the clangor of arms,
The drum rolls a peaceful hurrah.
'Tis cheering to think on the past,
'Tis cheering to think we've been true,
'Tis cheering to look on our stars and our stripes,
And gaze on our white, red, and blue.
Hurrah for the white, red, and blue,
Hurrah for the white, red, and blue.
'Tis cheering to look on our stars and our stripes,
And gaze on our white, red, and blue.

Here's a sigh for the brave that are dead,
Here's a sigh for the brave that are dead;
And who would not sigh for the glorious brave
That rest on a patriot bed?
'Tis glory, for country, to die,
'Tis glory that's solid and true;
'Tis glory to sleep 'neath our stars and our stripes,
And die for our white, red, and blue.
Hurrah for the white, red, and blue,
Hurrah for the white, red, and blue.
'Tis glory to sleep 'neath our stars and our stripes,
And die for the white, red, and blue.

Here's freedom of thought and of deed,
Here's freedom in valley and plain;
The first song of freedom that rose on our hills
Our seashore re-echoed again.
'Tis good to love country and friends,
'Tis good to be honest and true;
'Tis good to die shouting, on sea or on shore,
Hurrah for the white, red, and blue,
Hurrah for the white, red, and blue,
Hurrah for the white, red, and blue.
'Tis good to die shouting, on sea or on shore,
Hurrah for the white, red, and blue!

Union and Liberty.

[Air: "Crambambule."]

The Union, boys, it is our birthright—
For this we fight, for this we fight,
    For this we stand;
Its stars are still each freeman's birthright,
    So dearly loved, so dearly loved
    In all our land!
And we will still a nation be
For Union and for Liberty—
For Union and Liberty—
                We all agree!

The land we tread was sealed by martyrs,
Who've stood in line, who've stood in line
    On Freedom's field;
From ice-bound Maine to Oregon's waters
    There's not an inch, there's not an inch
    Their sons will yield!
And we shall still a nation be,
In Union and in Liberty—
For Union and Liberty—
                We all agree.

'Tis ours to shield our soil from danger,
And keep the flag, and keep the flag
    Of stars unfurled:
In Union, boys, lies all our grandeur,
    It makes us feared, it makes us feared
    Through all the world!
And we will, &c.

Let patriots all, in love united,
Like brothers stand, like brothers stand,
    Still side by side!
Eternal faith our fathers plighted;
    And curse the hand, and curse the hand
    That dares divide!
For we will still a nation be, &c.

Washington's Grave.

[Air: "The Grave of Bonaparte."]

Disturb not his slumbers, let Washington sleep
'Neath the boughs of the willow that over him weep;
His arm is unnerved, but his deeds remain bright
As the stars in the dark-vaulted heaven at night.
Oh! wake not the hero, his battles are o'er,
Let him rest undisturbed on Potomac's fair shore—
On the river's green border, so flowery drest,
With the hearts he loved fondly, LET WASHINGTON REST.
With the hearts he loved fondly, LET WASHINGTON REST.

Awake not his slumbers, tread lightly around—
'Tis the grave of the Freeman, 'tis Liberty's mound!
Thy name is immortal, our freedom ye won,
Brave sire of Columbia, our own Washington.
Oh! wake not the hero, his battles are o'er,
Let him rest, calmly rest, on his dear native shore,
While the stars and the stripes of our country shall wave
O'er the land that can boast of a WASHINGTON'S GRAVE.
O'er the land that can boast of a WASHINGTON'S GRAVE.

Reefing the Breakers.

(A Comic Recitation.)

The larboard leech of the topsail lines,
    Athwart the spritsail rigging runs;
The lanyard bows of the helm inclines
    To the windward lurch of the fok'sail guns,
The look-out boy at the tom-cat heads
    Espies on the watery waves a sail;
And the captain, as the galley he treads,
    Calls up all hands to reef the gale.

The starboard rail-blocks home are tacked,
    The binnacle close-reefed round is brought ;
The fore-top capstan clewlines backed
    To the prow of the bobstays, there made taut.
The skipper is heard from the gallant topmast,
    Through the close-tarred helm sheet comes the cry,
"Man the lee scuppers ! all hands avast !
    Tack spars ! reef breakers ! all stand by."

" Let go and reef, put your galley a-lee,
    Take a tack in the mizzenmast, quick, belay !"
Twas done, and the bulwarks once more free,
    Swung round till they tautened the main back-stay,
The dog-watch windlass abaft the caboose
    Was brought three points to the deadlight bow,
And once more the ship, from the port-holes loose,
    Flung her jib by the buntlines over her prow.

Her broadside now to the mainsail lays,
    The grog's served out in the spanker boom,
The breaker's reefed to the gang-plank ways,
    And again the stern sheets find sea room.
The thunders flash and the lightnings roar,
    The squall flies rushing from clew to clew ;
But the cat-head mate goes aloft once more,
    To lower the wheel to the eager crew.

"All hands ashore to luff the cleats !"
    And the lead is launched by the hard-a-lee ;
The pilot is hauled on the fore back sheets,
    And the fok'sail glides on the slackened sea.
Oh, dauntless crew ! oh, gallant ship !
    May you ever survive the leeward haul ;
May Neptune's figure-head bless your trip,
    And reefing the breakers end the squall.

The Sailor's Pride.

[Air: " The White Squall."]

The night was spent in mirth and glee,
When Ben was born upon the sea ;
He was the son of as brave a tar
As ever sailed in a man-of-war.
    All drank success to the ocean boy,
    Columbia's pride and our sailors' joy.

And when young Ben to manhood came,
He was crown'd with glory and with fame ;
In the battle's fierce heat he was seen,
Fighting the foe with dauntless mien.
    Then o'er his grog he would laugh and joke,
    And sing of Columbia's hearts of oak.

And when the ship into port did steer,
The sailors' hopes did soon appear ;
Their wives and sweethearts were in view,
To welcome home the gallant crew.
    Then the blue-eyed lass was soon espied
    By our gallant Ben, the sailors' pride.

The Frigate Constitution.

[Air : " Over the Water to Charley."]

Argo of Greece, that brought the fleece
    To the Thessalian city,
As we are told, by bards of old,
    Was sung in many a ditty ;
But Yankees claim a prouder name
    To spur their resolution,
Than Greece could boast and do her most—
    The frigate *Constitution*.

When first she press'd the stream's cool breast,
    Hope hail'd her pride of story;
Now she o'erpays hope's flatt'ring praise,
    By matchless deeds of glory;
Of all that roam the salt sea's foam,
    None floats to Neptune dearer,
Or fairer shines in fame's bright lines,
    Or more makes Britain fear her.

'Neath Hull's command, with a tough band,
    And nought beside to back her,
Upon a day, as log-books say,
    A fleet bore down to thwack her;
A fleet, you know, is odds or so,
    Against a single ship, sirs;
So cross the tide, her legs she tried,
    And gave the rogues the slip, sirs.

But time flies round, and soon she found
    While ploughing ocean's acres,
An even chance to join the dance,
    And turn keel up poor Dacres;
Dacres, 'tis clear, despises fear,
    Quite full of fun and prank is,
Hoists his ship's name, in playing game,
    Aloft to scare the Yankees.

On Brazil coast, she rul'd the roast,
    When Bainbridge was her captain;
Neat hammocks gave, made of the wave,
    Dead Britons to be wrapp'd in;
For there, in ire, 'midst smoke and fire,
    Her boys the *Java* met, sirs,
And in the fray her Yankee play
    Tipp'd Bull a *somerset*, sirs.

Next on deck, at fortune's beck,
    The dauntless Stewart landed;
A better tar ne'er shone in war,
    Or daring souls commanded;

Old *Ironsides* now once more rides
  In search of English cruisers ;
And Neptune grins, to see her twins,
  Got in an hour or two, sirs.

Then raise amain the joyful strain,
  For well she has deserv'd it,
Who brought the foe so often low,
  Cheer'd freedom's heart and nerv'd it ;
Long may she ride, our navy's pride,
  And spur to resolution ;
And seamen boast, and landsmen toast,
  The frigate *Constitution*.

The True Yankee Statesman.

[Air : "Harry Bluff."]

Charley Stewart, when a youth, left his land and his home,
In search of the foe on the ocean to roam,
Like a patriot his heart beat to liberty true,
And a foe to all tyrants the older he grew ;
His heart it was bold, and with valor 'twas warm ;
In his country's cause he the first was to arm,
To the wreck'd and distress'd oft his arm gave relief ;
And tho' rated a middy, he'd the skill of a chief,
  And the courage of a true Yankee seaman.

When, commander, promoted, the foe he'd pursue,
On old *Ironsides* long his striped banner flew ;
So true to his flag, and in battle so brave,
That he oft gave the proud foe a watery grave.
For his country he fought till with peace she was crown'd,
And now upon shore at the pen he is found ;
On the great ship of state may he next take command,
And her great *Constitution* safely steer on the land,
  With the mind of a true Yankee statesman.

E Pluribus Unum.

Though many and bright are the stars that appear
    In the flag of our country unfurl'd ;
And the stripes that are swelling in majesty there,
    Like a rainbow adorning the world ;
Their lights are unsullied as those in the sky
    By a deed that our fathers have done ;
And they're leagued in as true and as holy a tie
    In their motto of "Many in one."

From the hour when those patriots fearlessly flung
    That banner of starlight abroad,
Ever true to themselves, to that motto they clung
    As they clung to the promise of God ;
By the bayonet traced at the midnight of war,
    On the fields where our glory was won—
Oh ! perish the hand or the heart that would mar
    Our motto of "Many in one."

'Mid the smoke of the contest, the cannon's deep roar,
    How oft it hath gather'd renown ;
While those stars were reflected in rivers of gore
    When the cross and the lion went down.
And though few were their lights in the gloom of that hour,
    Yet the hearts that were striking below
Had God for their bulwark, and truth for their power,
    And they stopp'd not to number the foe.

We are many in one where there glitters a star
    In the blue of the heavens above ;
And tyrants shall quail 'mid their dungeons afar,
    When they gaze on our motto of love.
It shall gleam o'er the sea 'mid the bolts of the storm,
    O'er the tempest, and battle, and wreck,
And flame where our guns with their thunder grow warm,
    'Neath the blood on the slippery deck.

Then up with our flag, let it stream on the air,
   Though our fathers are cold in their graves ;   [dare,
They had hands that could strike, they had souls that could
   And their sons were not born to be slaves.
Up, up with our banner, where'er it may call,
   Our millions shall rally around ;
A nation of freemen that moment shall fall,
   When its stars shall be trailed on the ground.

The American Flag.

Proud flag of my country ! all gallantly streaming,
   In the breeze of the battle, when glory appears,
The stern scarlet blaze of its hurricane braving,
   While mercy hangs 'round with her olive and tears.
Proud flag of my country ! 'tis transport to meet
   Some smoke-colored hero who bled under thee,
As he rushed after victory's blood-dripping feet,
   And grasped the wild laurel that blossoms o'er the sea.

Yes, yes, if there's one whom a nation should love,
   One high-minded man, whom e'en angels admire,
It is he, who with spirit all flushed from above,
   With the rich loyal bloom of the patriot's fire,
Dares stand between danger and thee, all the hour
When the tyrant would tread on thy peace and thy power.

        Dares stand, &c.

The Heart that can Feel for Another.

(UPTON.)

Jack Steadfast and I were both messmates at sea,
   And plough'd half the world o'er together,
And many hot battles encounter'd have we,
   Strange climates, and all kinds of weather.
But seamen, you know, are inur'd to hard gales,
   Determin'd to stand by each other ;
And the boast of a tar, wheresoever he sails,
   Is the heart that can feel for another.

When often suspended 'twixt water and sky,
  And death yawn'd on all sides around us,
Jack Steadfast and I scorn'd to murmur or sigh,
  For danger could never confound us.
Smooth seas and rough billows to us were the same,
  Convinc'd we must brave one and t'other ;
And, like jolly sailors in life's chequer'd game,
  Give the heart that can feel for another.

Thus smiling at peril at sea or on shore,
  We box the old compass right cheerly !
Toss the can, boys, about—a word or two more,
  Yes, drink to the girls we lov'd dearly ;
For sailors, pray mind me, tho' strange kind of fish,
  Love the girls just as dear as their mother !
And, what's more, they love, what I hope you all wish,
  'Tis the heart that can feel for another.

Poor Jack.

(DIBDIN, 1811.)

Go patter to lubbers and swabs, d'ye see,
  'Bout danger, and fear, and the like ;
A tight-water boat and good sea room give me,
  And it ain't to a little I'll strike.
Though the tempest top-gallant masts smack smooth should smite,
  And shiver each splinter of wood,
Clear the wreck, stow the yards, and bouse everything tight,
  And under reef'd foresail we'll scud.
Avast, nor don't think me a milksop so soft,
  To be taken for trifles aback ;
For they say there's a Providence sits up aloft,
  To keep watch for the life of poor Jack.

Why, I heard the good chaplain palaver one day,
   About souls, heaven, mercy, and such,
And my timbers what lingo he'd coil·and belay,
   Why, 'twas just all as one as high Dutch;
But he said how a sparrow can't founder, d'ye see,
   Without orders that come down below;
And many fine things that proved clearly to me
   That Providence takes us in tow;
For, says he, do you mind me, let storms e'er so oft
   Take the top-sails of sailors aback;
There's a sweet little cherub sits perched up aloft,
   To keep watch for the life of poor Jack.

I said to our Poll, for, you see, she would cry,
   When last we weighed anchor for sea,
What argufies snivelling and piping your eye,
   Why, what a d—ned fool you must be!
Can't you see, the world's wide, and there's room for us all,
   Both for seamen and lubbers ashore;
And if to old Davy I should go, friend Poll,
   Why you never will hear of me more;
What then, all's a hazard—come, don't be so soft,
   Perhaps I may, laughing, come back;
For, d'ye see, there's a cherub sits smiling aloft,
   To keep watch for the life of poor Jack.

D'ye mind me, a sailor should be every inch
   All as one as a piece of the ship,
And with her, brave the world without off'ring to flinch,
   From the moment the anchor's a-trip;
As for me, in all weathers, all times, sides, and ends,
   Nought's a trouble from our duties that springs;
My heart is my Poll's, and my rhino my friend's,
   And as for my life, 'tis the country's!
Ev'n when my time comes, ne'er believe me so soft,
   As for grief to be taken aback;
That the same little cherub that sits up aloft
   Will look out for a good berth for poor Jack.

The Yankee Girls.

Not England's daughters, rosy-cheeked,
    Nor Scotia's lasses fair,
Nor Erin's blooming maidens, can
    With the Yankee girls compare ;
Though what they tell us of their charms
    All very true may be,
They'll not compare with Yankee girls—
    The Yankee girls for me.

Let Byron of Italian maids
    In glowing numbers sing,
And let the Turk his Georgian bride
    And black-eyed houris bring ;
Yet what they tell us of their charms
    All very true may be,
They'll not compare with Yankee girls—
    The Yankee girls for me.

Their faultless forms, their peerless eyes,
    As bright as morning dew !
Their cheeks so fair, their spirits light,
    Their hearts so warm and true !
They're chaste as fair, their minds unchanged,
    In thought and action free—
There's nothing like the Yankee girls—
    The Yankee girls for me.

Unto Columbia's daughters, then,
    We'll drain the goblet dry ;
Naught can the universe produce
    With the Yankee girls to vie.
Oh ! they're the fairest of the fair,
    And ever may they be—
There's nothing like the Yankee girls—
    The Yankee girls for me.

Long Live America!

[Air: "Gaily the Troubadour."]

Long live America,
    Land of the Free!
Firmly stand Freedom's land—
    Long life to thee!
Land where our fathers died
    For Liberty—
Land where their ashes are,
    Blessings on thee!

    CHORUS—Long live America, &c.

Brightly thy holy light
    Shines through the morn;
Soon shall its radiance
    All lands adorn!

    Long live America, &c.

As sands on ocean's shore
    Freemen abide,
Scattered thine empire o'er
    Thickly and wide!

    Long live America, &c.

May Faction ever sleep,
    Peace ever reign;
Hand-in-hand freemen stand,
    Rights to maintain!

    Long live America, &c.

May streams of knowledge flow
    Throughout the land—
Thus shall the light of life
    All minds expand.

    Long live America, &c.

God save America!
  Oh, may she be
O'ershadow'd evermore,
  Father, by Thee!

    Long live America, &c.

America! Bright name;
  In strength and pride
Blaze thine altar flame
  'Tween the ocean's tide.

    Long live America, &c.

Bright home of Freedom's shrine,
  May'st thou e'er be
Guided by power divine —
  Long life to thee!

    Long live America, &c.

Stand by the Flag.

Stand by the flag, its folds have stream'd in glory,
  To foes a fear, to friends a vestal robe.
And spread in rhythmic lines the sacred story
  Of freedom's triumphs over all the globe;
Stand by the flag, on land, and ocean billow;
  By it your fathers stood, unmoved and true;
Living, defended; dying, from their pillow,
  With their last blessing, pass'd it on to you.

Stand by the flag, though death-shots round it rattle;
  And underneath its waving folds have met,
In all the dread array of sanguine battle,
  The quivering lance and glittering bayonet;
Stand by the flag, all doubt and treason scorning,
  Believe, with courage firm and faith sublime,
That it will float until the eternal morning
  Pales in its glories all the lights of time.

The American Tar.

[Air: " The American Star."]

The goddess of freedom borne down by oppression,
  In Europe's fam'd regions no longer found rest ;
She wept at the heart-rending wide desolation,
  And languishing look'd for relief from the West.
She heard that Columbia was rearing a temple,
  Where she should be worship'd in peace and in war ;
Old Neptune confirm'd it, cried Lo ; here's a sample,
  Presenting with pride an American Tar.

Cease weeping, then, goddess, to thee I've consigned him,
  He loves thee and he thy protector will be ;
Believe me a more gallant youth you will find him,
  Than ever bore your banners through ocean or sea.
When his galley he trims, firm resolved for the onset,
  Wo ! wo ! to that foe, who his prowess will dare,
Long will his country lament, that he e'er went
  And brav'd the avenging American Tar.

He boasts not, but firm as the oak of his forest,
  Serene as a calm ; but fierce as a storm,
When wild roars the battle you'll find him the foremost ;
  When victor, the prostrate protecting from harm.
And I have decreed, he's so gallant a fellow,
  O'er my wide dominions he shall be a star
Will light you in triumph, o'er ev'ry billow,
  His name, listen angel ! American Tar.

The American Flag.

(JOSEPH RODMAN DRAKE, 1795–1820.)

When Freedom from her mountain height
  Unfurled her standard to the air,
She tore the azure robe of night,
  And set the stars of glory there.
She mingled with its gorgeous dyes
The milky baldrick of the skies,

And striped its pure celestial white
With streakings of the morning light ;
Then from his mansion in the sun
She called her eagle-bearer down,
And gave into his mighty hand
The symbol of her chosen land.

Majestic monarch of the cloud,
  Who rear'st aloft thy regal form
To hear the tempest-trumpings loud,
  And see the lightning-lances driven ;
When stride the warriors of the storm,
And rolls the thunder-drum of heaven !
Child of the sun ! to thee 'tis given
  To guard the banner of the free !
To hover in the sulphur smoke,
To ward away the battle stroke,
And bid its blendings shine afar,
Like rainbows on the cloud of war—
  The harbingers of victory !

Flag of the brave, thy folds shall fly,
The sign of hope and triumph high,
When speaks the signal trumpet tone,
And the long line comes gleaming on ;
Ere yet the life-blood, warm and wet,
Has dimmed the glistening bayonet,
Each soldier eye shall brightly turn
To where thy sky-born glories burn,
And, as his springing steps advance,
Catch war and vengeance from the glance.
And when the cannon-mouthings loud
Heave in wild wreaths the battle-shroud,
And gory sabres rise and fall,
Like shoots of flame on midnight's pall,
Then shall thy meteor-glances glow,
  And cowering foes shall sink beneath
Each gallant arm that strikes below
  That lovely messenger of death.

Flag of the seas! on ocean wave
Thy stars shall glitter o'er the brave;
When death, careering on the gale,
Sweeps darkly round the bellied sail,
And frighted waves rush wildly back
Before the broadside's reeling rack,
Each dying wanderer of the sea
Shall look at once to Heaven and thee,
And smile to see thy splendors fly
In triumph o'er his closing eye.
Flag of the free heart's hope and home,
  By angel hands to valor given,
Thy stars have lit the welkin dome,
  And all thy hues were born in Heaven.
Forever float that standard sheet!
  Where breathes the foe but falls before us,
With freedom's soil beneath our feet,
  And freedom's banner streaming o'er us?

The Ocean Hero.

[Air: "The Star-Spangled Banner."]

Wake, sons of Columbia, wake gratitude's lay,
  And sing of great Stewart, our bold ocean hero,
Who led forth our tars to break tyranny's sway,
  And drive from our coast every plundering Nero.
      In youth's early hour,
      The seas he did scour,
And fought with Decatur, 'gainst Tripoli's power;
He taught them that freemen their life's blood will drain,
Their trade to protect and their rights to maintain.

When the barks of proud Britain came over the main,
  To plunder our ships and impress our bold seamen,
'Twas he roused our navy and steered forth again,
  And dealt to our foemen the vengeance of freemen.
      Oh, he humbled their pride,
      By his tough *Ironsides*,
And he lower'd *Levant* and *Cyane* with the tide,
Then long life to Stewart, and long may he stand,
The pride of our navy, the chief of our land.

Our Man-of-War.

How gallantly our battle-ship
  O'er foam-crest surges flies,
Her white wings skimming now the sea,
  Now soaring to the skies.
Her flag of light's a meteor bright,
  That heeds no storm or wreck,
A thousand patriot spirits share
  The glory of her deck.

Adieu to home, where loved ones dwell,
  Our country quick we leave;
Hark to the deep cathedral swell
  Of th' outward bounding wave!
A sigh for friends now far behind,
  A cheer for honor's way;
Three more, for majesty of mind,
  And freedom's boundless sway.

Farewell awhile, thou lessening shore
  All hail thou mighty sea!
That bears our pennant proud where'er
  A foeman's flag we see.
Lo! on th' horizon looms a hull
  Whose black spars hostile rise;
But umpire now, thou ocean great;
  Be witnesses, you skies.

Mark! moving like a spirit dark,
  That warship lurches now;
Clear decks for action! To your guns,
  Steadily! each gallant brow!
See! see! she hoists the foe's red flag!
  Up with our stripes and stars!
His bow gun booms! He fires again!
  Have at him, Yankee tars?

Well done ! bear down upon him, lads,
  Launch forth your iron fires !
As Perry, Hall, Decatur did,
  Now emulate your sires !
Hurrah ! but see, he strikes his flag,
  Cease firing ! we must save
His crippled ship—she sinks, bear a hand
  To rescue the conquer'd brave.

Soon on our deck the sullen foe
  Surrenders his command,
The fight is o'er, now foes no more,
  We grasp the friendly hand.
Victors ! we soothe his wounded pride,
  Thus brave men ever meet ;
And Erie, Tunis, Champlain prove
  That such tars man our fleet.

Oh ! be it ever o'er such men
  That our striped banner flows,
Full glorious, when the war-wind's hush'd,
  Or when it fiercely blows.
Come, cheer all hands ! we're homeward bound,
  For peace and altars free ;
The motto, " Don't give up the ship ! "
  Your watchward ever be.

Then crowd all sail ! our trim, taut ship
  For home and loved ones steer,
And all our household deities,
  Whose magic spells are dear.
Let discipline be still observed,
  As e'er our seaman's boast ;
Hark ! hark ! Columbia greets us back,
  To guard her rock-girt coast.

Bainbridge's Tid-re I.

Come, lads, draw near,
And you shall hear,
In truth as chaste as Dian, O!
How Bainbridge true,
And his bold crew,
Again have tamed the lion, O!
'Twas off Brazil,
He got the pill,
Which made him cry PECCAVI, O!
But hours two
The *Java* new,
Maintain'd the battle bravely, O!

But our gallant Yankee tars as soon as they were piped to quarters, gave three cheers, and boldly swore by the blood of the heroes of Tripoli, that sooner than strike, they'd go to the bottom singing—Tid-re I, &c.

Now Johnny Bull,
All canvas full,
Bore down upon us cheerily, O!
While we kept snug
As bug in rug
Till half gun-shot or nearly, O!
We show'd our stripes,
Gave John the gripes,
They sent him pills in plenty, O!
Which dosed him well,
As he can tell,
Our doctors all being ready, O.

O! it would have done your heart good to have seen how nimbly our little spitfires were set to work and what a dust they kicked up in poor Johnny's quarters. We could soon observe how the matter would turn out. "Stick to them, my boys!" says the commodore. "Huzza!" sung out the crew, "we'll conquer or die!" For every soul on board, even down to the smallest powder-monkey, was determined to give them a complete bit of—Tid-re I, &c.

　　　　Now close engaged,
　　　　The battle raged,
　Both being as tough as hickory, O!
　　　　But still we swore
　　　　We'd ne'er give o'er,
　Till we had gained the victory, O!
　　　　Round shot and bars
　　　　Soon cut her spars,
　And well we slash'd her rigging, O!
　　　　Nul after nul,
　　　　We plugged her hull,
　Her bowsprit too went jigging, O!

　　O, swamp it, if you had only seen how we plumped her between wind and water, and how our grape-shot rattled in at her port-holes, while her yards flew about their ears like straws in a high wind. We soon saw they were in a nation fluster, while our Yankee boys kept cool and steady, still bravely keeping up their—Tid-re I, &c.

　　　　One hour was past,
　　　　When now a mast,
　Close by the board went o'er, O!
　　　　Our gunner cries,
　　　　"My jolly boys,
　Escape us now she'll never, O!
　　　　Point well each gun,
　　　　We'll show them fun,
　Her ensign down she soon will haul;
　　　　We'd give them play,
　　　　This glorious day,
　Shall make them quick for quarter call."

　　So at it we stuck, pell mell, like good fellows, and we made such a nation clatter with them sweeping guns, that we could hardly hear anything for the rotten noise, but our gunner watched her close and touched off our Yankee barkers so neatly in time, that slap dab every shot struck her somewhere, which soon made them feel that Yankee tars knew very well how to pay them a—Tid-re I, &c.

    We plied her well
    At every swell,
  And fast her men were killing, O!
    And though so fast,
    Went every mast,
  To strike she seem'd not willing, O!
    But to her cost,
    She found at last,
  To longer fight us wouldn't do;
    For Yankee tars,
    Who knew no fears,
  To conquer now she couldn't, O!

  So when the firing ceased on both sides, we had time to look about us, but we could hardly believe our eyes, for she lay like a log upon the water, there was not a stump standing higher than the pump in father's schooner, and her sides looked for all the world like mother's cullender; so completely had we peppered her. So to work went the boats, and aboard came the prisoners; then the commodore gave orders to burn the prize; "for," says he, "my brave boys, any attempt to tow her into port would be a—Tid-re I," &c.

    So now, my hearts,
    We've played our parts,
  Proud John once more we've humbled!
    It may be said,
    A Bull he made
  On Yankees when he stumbled, O!
    We'll let him see
    We'll still be free,
  In spite of all his boasting, O!
    And if he comes
    To run his hums,
  We'll give proud John a roasting, O!

  So now, my lads, fill up the cans, to the health of all our brave commanders; and while we remember with pride the glorious victories we have gained, let us be resolved, one and all, still to maintain the honor of our flag, and Johnny Bull will soon find that any attempt to conquer a nation of Freemen will be all a—Tid-re I, &c.

Perry's Victory; or, The Battle of Lake Erie.

September 10th, 1813.

[Air: "Admiral Benbow."]

We sail'd to and fro in Erie's broad lake,
To find British bullies, or get in their wake,
When we hoisted our canvas with true Yankee speed,
And the brave Captain Perry our squadron did lead.

We sail'd through the lake, boys, in search of the foe,
In the cause of Columbia our bravery to show,
To be equal in combat was all our delight,
As we wished the proud Britons to know we could fight.

And whether like Yeo, boys, they'd taken affright,
We could see not, nor find them by day or by night,
So a-cruising we went in a glorious cause,
In defense of our rights, our freedom, and laws.

At length to our liking six sails hove in view,
Huzza! says brave Perry, Huzza! says his crew,
And then for the chase, boys, with our brave little crew,
We fell in with the bullies and gave them burgeau.

Though the force was unequal, determin'd to fight,
We brought them to action before it was night;
We let loose our thunder, our bullets did fly,
"Give them your shots, boys," our commander did cry.

We gave them a broadside, our cannon to try,
"Well done," says brave Perry, "for quarters they'll cry;
Shoot well home, my brave boys they shortly shall see,
That as brave as they are, still braver are we."

Then we drew up our squadron, each man full of fight,
And put the proud Britons in a terrible plight,
The brave Perry's movements will prove fully as bold
As the fam'd Admiral Nelson's prowess of old.

The conflict was sharp, boys, each man to his gun,
For our country, her glory, the vict'ry was won,
So six sail (the whole fleet) was our fortune to take.
Here's a health to brave Perry who governs the Lake.

Destruction of Tea, 1776.

[Air: " Hosier's Ghost."]

As near beauteous Boston lying,
  On the gently swelling flood,
Without Jack or pendant flying,
  Three ill-fated tea ships rode.

Just as glorious Sol was setting,
  On the wharf a numerous crew,
Sons of Freedom, fear forgetting,
  Suddenly appeared in view.

Armed with hammer, axe, and chisels,
  Weapons now for warlike deed,
Towards the herbage-freighted vessels
  They approached with dreadful speed.

O'er their heads, in lofty mid-sky,
  Three bright angel-forms were seen,
This was Hampden, that was Sidney,
  With fair Liberty between.

"Soon," they cried, "our foes you'll banish,
  Soon thy triumph shall be won;
Scarce shall setting Phœbus vanish,
  Ere the deathless deed be done."

Quick as thought the ships were boarded,
  Hatches burst and chests displayed,
Axes, hammers, help accorded,
  What a glorious crash they made!

Squash, into the deep descended,
  Cursed weed of China's coast,
Thus at once our fears were ended!
  British rights shall dear be lost.

Captains! once more hoist your streamers,
  Spread your sails, and plough the wave,
Tell your masters they were dreamers
  When they thought to cheat the brave.

Bonne Homme Richard and Serapis.

September 23d, 1779.

[Air: "Can I Forget to Love Thee, Mary?"]

O'er the rough main with flowing sheet,
The guardian of a numerous fleet;
  Serapis from the Baltic came;
A ship of less tremendous force
Sail'd by her side, the self-same course—
  Countess of Scarborough was her name.

And now their native coasts appear,
Britannia's hills their summits rear
  Above the German main;
Fond to suppose their dangers o'er,
They southward coast along the shore,
  Thy waters, gentle Thames, to gain.

Full forty guns *Serapis* bore,
And *Scarborough's Countess* twenty-four,
   Mann'd with Old England's bravest tars;
What flag that rides the Gallic seas
Shall dare attack such piles as these,
   Design'd for tumult and for wars?

Now, from the topmast's giddy height,
A seaman cried, " Four sail in sight
   Approach with favoring gales."
Pearson, resolved to save the fleet,
Stood off to sea these ships to meet,
   And closely braced his shivering sails.

With him advanced the *Countess* bold,
Like a black tar in wars grown old;
   And now these floating piles drew nigh;
But muse, unfold, what chief of fame
In the other warlike squadron came,
   Whose standards at his mast-heads fly?

'Twas Jones, brave Jones, to battle led
As bold a crew as ever bled
   Upon the sky-surrounded main;
The standards of the Western world
Were to the willing winds unfurl'd,
   Denying Britain's tyrant reign.

The *Good Man Richard* led the line,
The *Alliance* next; with these combine
   The Gallic ship they *Pallas* call;
The *Vengeance*, arm'd with sword and flame,
These to attack the Britons came;
   But TWO accomplish'd all.

Now Phœbus sought his pearly bed;
But who can tell the scenes of dread,
   The horrors of that fatal night?
Close up these floating castles came;
The *Good Man Richard* bursts in flame;
   Serapis trembled at the sight.

She felt the fury of her ball ;
Down, prostrate down the Britons fall;
   The decks were strew'd with slain ;
Jones to the foe his vessel lash'd,
And while the black artillery flashed,
   Loud thunders shook the main.

Alas ! that mortals should employ
Such murdering engines to destroy
   That frame by Heaven so nicely joined ;
Alas ! that ever God decreed
That brother should by brother bleed,
   And pour such madness in the mind.

But thou, brave Jones, no blame shall bear,
The rights of man demand your care ;
   For these you dare the greedy waves.
No tyrant on destruction bent
Has plann'd thy conquests ; thou art sent
   To humble tyrants and their slaves.

See ! dread *Serapis* flames again !
And art thou, Jones, among the slain,
   And sunk to Neptune's caves below?
He lives ; though crowds around him fall,
Still he, unhurt, survives them all ;
   Almost alone he fights the foe.

And can your ship these strokes sustain?
Behold your brave companions slain,
   All clasp'd in ocean's cold embrace !
"Strike or be sunk," the Briton cries,
"Sink if you can," the chief replies,
   Fierce lightnings blazing in his face.

Then to the side three guns he drew,
(Almost deserted by his crew),
   And charged them deep with woe ;
By Pearson's flash he aim'd hot balls ;
His main-mast totters - down it falls,
   O'erwhelming half below.

Pearson had yet disdained to yield,
But scarce his secret fears conceal'd,
   And thus was heard to cry:
"With hell, not mortals, I contend,
What art thou—human, or a fiend,
   That dost my force defy?"

"Return, my lads, the fight renew!"
So call'd bold Pearson to his crew,
   But call'd, alas! in vain;
Some on the decks lay maim'd and dead;
Some to their deep recesses fled,
   And hosts were shrouded in the main.

Distress'd, forsaken, and alone,
He haul'd his tattered standard down,
   And yielded to his gallant foe;
Bold *Pallas* soon the *Countess* took—
Thus both their haughty colors struck,
   Confessing what the brave can do.

But Jones, too dearly didst thou buy
These ships, possess'd so gloriously;
   Too many deaths disgraced the fray;
Your bark that bore the conquering flame
That the proud Briton overcame,
   Even she forsook thee on thy way.

For when the morn began to shine,
Fatal to her—the ocean brine,
   Pour'd through each spacious wound;
Quick in the deep she disappear'd;
But Jones to friendly Belgia steer'd,
   With conquest and with glory crown'd.

Go on, great man, to scourge the foe,
And bid these haughty Britons know,
   They to our "Thirteen Stars" shall bend;
The Stars that, clad in dark attire,
Long glimmered with a feeble fire,
   But radiant now ascend.

Bend to the Stars that flaming rise
On Western world's more brilliant skies,
   Fair Freedom's reign restor'd ;
So, when the Magi came from far,
Beheld the God-attending star,
   They trembled and adored.

The Stripe and the Star.

[Air : "How Happy's the Soldier."]

Where lordly Champlain, on its wild surging wave,
Bears proudly the keels of the free and the brave,
Unmoved by the boasts which their courage decry,
Our fleet's gallant pennons in buoyancy fly,
Though Albion in thunder descend, and her war
Break rough o'er the sons of the Stripe and the Star.

O'er her white foamy bosom, with shouts of delight,
The sons of Columbia rush fearless to fight ;
A hero presides o'er the battle deck brave,
And the flag of Macdonough sweeps broad o'er the wave,
Where Freedom above, cheering smiles from her car,
And the laurel-wreaths twine round the Stripe and the Star.

No longer ye Island-born sons of the sea,
Unequal, contend with the brave and the free,
Where Liberty scoffs at your vaunts and your pride,
And her conquest-crown'd navies in victory ride,
But bow your proud heads, as ye skulk from the war,
And bend to the sheen of the Stripe and the Star.

Paul Jones.

[Air: "Star-Spangled Banner."]

A song unto Liberty's brave Buccaneer,
  Ever bright be the fame of the patriot Rover,
For our rights he first fought in his "black privateer,"
  And faced the proud foe ere our sea they cross'd over,
    In their channel and coast,
    He scattered their host,
And proud Briton robbed of her sea-ruling boast,
And her rich merchants' barks shunned the ocean in fear
Of Paul Jones, fair Liberty's brave Buccaneer.

In the first fleet that sailed in defense of our land,
  Paul Jones forward stood to defend freedom's arbor,
He led the bold *Alfred* at Hopkin's command,
  And drove the fierce foeman from Providence harbor,
    'Twas his hand that raised,
    The first flag that blazed,*
And his deeds 'neath the "Pine tree" all ocean amaz'd
For hundreds of foes met a watery bier,
From Paul Jones, fair Liberty's bold Buccaneer.

His arm crushed the tory and mutinous crew,
  That strove to have freemen inhumanly butchered;
Remember his valor at proud Flamborough,
  Where he made the bold *Serapis* strike to the *Richard;*
    Oh! he robbed of their store
    The vessel sent o'er
To feed all the tories and foes on our shore,
He gave freemen the spoils and long may they revere
The name of fair Liberty's bold Buccaneer.

---

* The first flag of the Revolution was raised by Paul Jones' own hand, on board the *Alfred* on the Delaware River, in 1776. It was a Pine tree, having a rattlesnake coiled at the root of it, with the motto, "Don't tread on me."—*See Cooper's Naval History.*

Hurrah for the Sea.

A bold, brave crew, on an ocean blue,
  And a ship that loves the blast,
With a good wind piping merrily,
  In the tall and gallant mast.
    Ha! ha! my boys,
    These are the joys
  Of the noble and the brave,
    Who love a life
    In the tempest strife,
  And a home on the mountain wave.

When the driving rain of the hurricane
  Puts the light of the light-house out,
And the growling thunder sound is going
  On the whirlwind's battle rout.
    Ha! ha! do you think
    That the valiant shrink?
  No! no! we are bold and brave,
    And we love to fight
    In the wild midnight,
  With the storm on the mountain wave.

Breezes that die where the green woods sigh,
  To the landsmen sweet may be,
But give to the brave the broad-backed wave
  And the tempest's midnight glee!
    Ha! ha! the blast,
    And the bending mast,
  And the sea wind brisk and cold,
    And the thunder's jar
    On the seas afar,
  Are things that suit the bold.

The timbers creak, the sea birds shriek,
　There's lightning in the blast!
Hard to the leeward, mariners,
　For the storm is gathering fast;
　　Ha! ha! to-night,
　　Boys, we must fight,
　But the winds which o'er us yell
　　Shall never scare
　　The mariner
　In his winged citadel.

The Lass that Loves a Sailor.

(DIBDIN.)

The moon on the ocean was dimm'd by a ripple,
　Affording a chequer'd light;
The gay jolly tars pass'd the word for a tipple
　And the toast, for 'twas Saturday night;
　　Some sweetheart or wife,
　　He loved as his life,
Each drank, and he wish'd he could hail her;
　　But the standing toast
　　That pleased the most,
　　Was the wind that blows
　　The ship that goes,
And the lass that loves a sailor.

Some drank his country, and some her brave ships,
　And some the *Constitution;*
Some, may the French, and all such rips,
　Yield to American resolution.
　　That fate may bless
　　Some Poll or Bess,
　And that they soon might hail;
Some drank the navy, and some our land,
　This glorious land of freedom;

Some that our tars may never want
  Heroes brave to lead them.
That she who's in distress may find
  Such friends that ne'er shall fail her.
    But the standing toast, &c.

Tom Bowling.

(DIBDIN.)

Here a sheer hulk lies poor Tom Bowling,
  The darling of our crew,
No more he'll hear the tempest howling,
  For death has brought him to.
His form was of the manliest beauty,
  His heart was kind and soft;
Faithful below he did his duty,
  And now he is gone aloft.

Tom never from his word departed,
  His virtues were so rare,
His friends were many and true-hearted,
  His Poll was kind and fair!
And then he sang so blythe and jolly,
  Ah! many's the time and oft;
But mirth has changed to melancholy,
  For Tom is gone aloft.

Yet shall poor Tom find pleasant weather
  When He who all commands
Shall give (to call life's crew together)
  The word to pipe all hands.
Thus death who kings and tars despatches,
  In vain Tom's life has doff'd;
For tho' his body's under hatches,
  His soul has gone aloft.

Black-Eyed Susan.

(JOHN GAY, 1688-1732.)

All in the Downs the fleet was moor'd,
   The streamers waving in the wind,
When black-eyed Susan came on board,
   Oh! where shall I my true love find?
Tell me, ye jovial sailors, tell me true,
Does my sweet William sail among your crew?

William, who high upon the yard,
   Rock'd by the billows to and fro,
Soon as her well-known voice he heard,
   He sigh'd and cast his eyes below;
The cord slides quickly through his glowing hands,
And quick as lightning on the deck he stands.

So the sweet lark, high pois'd in air,
   Shuts close his pinions to his breast,
(If chance his mate's shrill note he hear,)
   And drops at once into her nest;
The noblest captain in the British fleet
Might envy William's lips those kisses sweet.

O, Susan! Susan! lovely dear!
   My vows shall ever true remain;
Let me kiss off that falling tear,
   We only part to meet again.
Change as ye list, ye winds, my hope shall be
The faithful compass that still points to thee.

Believe not what the landsmen say,
   Who tempt with doubts thy constant mind;
They'll tell thee, sailors, when away,
   In every port a mistress find;
Yes, yes, believe them when they tell thee so,
For thou art present wheresoe'er I go.

If to far India's coast we sail,
  Thy eyes are seen in diamonds bright;
Thy breath is Afric's spicy gale,
  Thy skin is ivory so white;
Thus every beauteous object that I view,
Wakes in my soul some charms of lovely Sue.

Tho' battles call me from thy arms,
  Let not my pretty Susan mourn;
Tho' cannon roar, yet safe from harm,
  William shall to his dear return;
Love turns aside the balls that round me fly,
Lest precious tears should drop from Susan's eye.

The boatswain gave the dreadful word,
  The sails their swelling bosom spread;
No longer must she stay on board;
  They kiss'd; she sigh'd; he hung his head,
Her less'ning boat unwilling rows to land,
Adieu! she cries, and waves her lily hand.

Heaving the Lead.

For England, when, with fav'ring gale,
  Our gallant ship up channel steer'd,
And scudding under easy sail,
  The high blue western land appear'd
To heave the lead the seaman sprung,
And to the pilot cheerily sung,
  " By the deep—NINE!"

And bearing up to gain the port,
  Some well-known object kept in view,
An abbey-tower, a harbor fort,
  Or beacon, to the vessel true;
While oft the lead the seaman flung,
And to the pilot cheerily sung,
  " By the mark—SEVEN!"

As the much-loved shore we near,
  With transport we behold the roof
Where dwelt a friend or partner dear,
  Of faith and love a matchless proof.
The lead once more the seaman flung,
And to the watchful pilot sung,
    "Quarter less—FIVE!"

Now to her berth the ship draws nigh,
  With slack'ning sail she feels the tide;
Stand clear the cable, is the cry,
  The anchor's gone, we safely ride.
The watch is set, and through the night
We hear the seamen with delight
Proclaim—"ALL'S WELL!"

Stand to Your Guns.

Stand to your guns, my hearts of oak,
Let not a word be spoke,
Victory soon will crown the joke;
  Be silent and be ready.
Ram home your guns and sponge them well,
Let us be sure the balls will tell,
The cannon's roar shall sound their knell,
  Be steady, boys, be steady.

Nor yet—nor yet—reserve your fire,
I do desire :—Fire ;
Now the elements do rattle,
The gods, amazed, behold the battle!
  A broadside, my boys!

See the blood in purple tide,
Trickle down her battered side ;
Winged with fate her bullets fly ;
Conquer, boys, or bravely die,
Hurl destruction on your foes,
  She sinks—huzza !
To the bottom down she goes.

Bound 'Prentice to a Waterman.

Bound 'prentice to a waterman, I larn'd a bit to row,
  But bless your heart I always was so gay,
That to treat a little water-nymph, that took my heart in tow,
  I run'd myself in debt a bit, and then I run'd away.
      Singing ri tol, fol de rol, yo ho.

Board a man-of-war I enter'd next and larn'd to quaff good flip,
  And from home we scudded on so gay,
I ran my rigs, but liked so well my captain, crew, and ship,
  That come what will, blow me if I'll ever run away.
      Singing ri tol, &c.

With glee I've sail'd the world all round and larn'd a bit to fight,
  But, somehow, I was a prisoner ta'en;
So when the mounseer gaoler to my dungeon show'd a light,
  Blinded both his peepers, and then ran away again.
      Singing ri tol, &c.

I've ran many risks in life, on ocean and on shore,
  And always like a Yankee got the day;
And fighting in Columbia's cause, will run as many more,
  And let me face ten thousand foes, will never run away.
      Singing ri, tol, &c.

We Tars Have a Maxim.

We tars have a maxim, your honor, d'ye see,
  To live in the same way we fight;
We never give in; and when running a-lee,
  We pipe hands the vessel to light
It may do for a lubber to snivel, and that,
  If by chance on a shoal he is cast,
But a tar, among breakers or thrown on a flat,
  Pulls away, tug-and-tug, to the last.
      With a yeo, yeo, yeo, fol de rol, lol de lol.

This life, as we are told, is a kind of a cruise,
  In which storms and calms take their turn ;
If it's storm, why we bustle ; if calm, then we loose
  All taut from the stem to the stern.
Our captain, who in our own lingo would speak,
  Would say to the cable, stick fast ;
And whether the anchor be cast, or a-peak,
  Pull away, tug-and-tug, to the last.

    With a yeo, &c.

Behold! How Brightly.

(Opera of " Massaniello.")

Behold! how brightly breaks the morning,
  Though bleak our lot, our hearts are warm ;
To toil inured, all danger scorning ;
  We hail the breeze or brave the storm.
    Put off, put off, our course we know ;
    Take heed, take heed, whisper low ;
    Look out and spread your nets with care,
  The prey we seek we'll soon, we'll soon ensnare.

    Put off, &c.

Away, though tempests darken o'er us,
  Boldly, still we'll stem the wave,
Hoist, hoist all sail, while shines before us
  Hope's beacon light to cheer the brave.
    Put off, put off, our course we know ;
    Take heed, take heed, and whisper low,
    Look out and spread your nets with care,
  The prey we seek we'll soon, we'll soon ensnare.

    Put off, &c.

While all on shore are soundly sleeping,
　Our little bark we'll gaily trim ;
And whilst the beacon watch is keeping,
　We'll gaily chaunt our morning hymn.
　　Through waters deep we'll swiftly glide,
　　And silent keep, and silent keep ;
　　For He who rules the angry tide
　　Is King o'er the deep, is King o'er the deep.

　　　Through waters, &c.

Constitution and Guerriere.

August 13th, 1812.

[Air : " The Landlady of France."]

　　It oft times has been told,
　　That British seamen bold,
Could flog the tars of France so neat and handy, oh !
　　But they never found their match,
　　Till the Yankees did them catch,
Oh, the Yankee boys, for fighting, are the dandy, oh !

　　The *Guerriere*, a frigate bold,
　　On the foaming ocean roll'd,
Commanded by proud Dacres, the grandee, oh !
　　With a choice of British crew,
　　As a rammer ever drew,
They could flog the French, two to one so handy, oh !

　　When this frigate hove in view,
　　Says proud Dacres to his crew,
Come, clear the ship for action, and be handy, oh !
　　To the weather gauge, boys, get her,
　　And to make his men fight better,
Gave them to drink, gunpowder mixed with brandy, oh !

Then, Dacres loudly cries,
Make this Yankee ship your prize,
You can in thirty minutes, neat and handy, oh!
Thirty-five's enough I'm sure,
And if you'll do it in a score,
I'll treat you to a double share of brandy, oh!

The British shot flew hot,
Which the Yankees answered not,
Till they got within the distance they call handy, oh!
Now, says Hull unto his crew,
Boys, let's see what we can do,
If we take this boasting Briton we're the dandy, oh!

The first broadside we pour'd,
Carried her mainmast by the board,
Which made this lofty frigate look abandon'd, oh!
Then Dacres shook his head,
And to his officers he said,
Lord, I didn't think these Yankees were so handy, oh!

Our second told so well,
That their fore and mizzen fell,
Which dous'd the royal ensign neat and handy, oh!
By George, says he, we're done,
And then fired a lee gun,
While the Yankees struck up Yankee Doodle Dandy, oh!

Then Dacres came on board
To deliver up his sword,
Loth was he to part with it, so handy, oh!
Oh, keep your sword, says Hull,
For it only makes you dull,
So cheer up, come, let us have a little brandy, oh!

Come, fill your glasses full,
And we'll drink to Captain Hull,
And so merrily we'll push about the brandy, oh!
John Bull may toast his fill,
Let the world say what it will,
But the Yankee boys for fighting are the dandy oh!

The Life of a Tar.

The life of a tar is the life I love ;
The sea is beneath us, the heavens above ;
Our reign undisputed from the sky to the sea,
Whose life can compare to the mariner free ;
When winds whistle loud, still in safety we ride,
Through waves which ne'er whelm as we merrily ride,
No life half so happy, no life half so free,
While we skim undismay'd o'er the rolling sea.

The hope of our maidens, the pride of our home,
His heart is a stranger to falsehood and guile ;
His ship is his home, his nation the world,
His boast is his flag, never wrongly unfurl'd ;
His heart his true honor—how happy is he,
While he skims undismay'd o'er the rolling sea,
No life half so happy, no life half so free,
While he skims undismay'd o'er the rolling sea.

Steady She Goes.

The Yankee tar no danger knows,
    But fearless braves the angry deep,
The ship's his cradle of repose,
    And sweetly rocks him to his sleep ;
He, though the raging surges swell,
      In his hammock swings,
      When the steersman sings,
Steady she goes! all's well.

While on the topsail-yard he springs,
    Columbia's vessel heaves in view,
He asks, but she no letter brings
    From bonny Kate he loved so true ;

Then sighs he for his native dell;
    Yet to hope he clings,
      While the steersman sings,
Steady she goes! all's well.

The storm is past, the battle's o'er,
   Nature and man repose in peace,
Then homeward bound, on Columbia's shore,
   The hope of joys that ne'er will cease;
His Kate's sweet voice those joys foretell,
    And his big heart springs,
      As the steersman sings,
Steady she goes! all's well.

The Sailor's Last Whistle.

Whether sailor or not, for a moment avast,
Poor Jack's mizzen-topsail is laid to the mast,
He'll never turn out, or more heave the lead,
He's now all aback, nor will sails shoot ahead;
Yet though worms gnaw his timbers, his vessel's a wreck,
When he hears the last whistle, he'll jump upon deck.

Secured, in his cabin, he's moored in his grave,
Nor hears any more the loud roar of the wave;
Pressed by death, he is sent to the tender below,
Where seamen and lubbers must every one go.

    Yet though worms, &c.

With his frame a mere hulk, and his reckoning on board,
At length he dropped down to mortality's road;
With eternity's ocean before him in view,
He cheerfully pops out, My messmates, adieu!

    Yet though worms, &c.

A Wet Sheet and a Flowing Sea.

(ALLAN CUNNINGHAM.)

A wet sheet and a flowing sea,
  And a wind that follows fast,
And fills the white and rustling sail,
  And bends the gallant mast;
And bends the gallant mast, my boys!
  While like an eagle free,
Away our good ship flies, and leaves
  Columbia on our lee.

    Oh, give me a wet sheet, a flowing sea,
      A wind that follows fast,
    And fills the white and rustling sail,
      And bends the gallant mast.

O! For a soft and gentle wind,
  I heard a fair one cry;
But give to me the roaring breeze,
  And white waves heaving high;
And white waves heaving high, my boy!
  The good ship tight and free;
The world of waters is our home,
  And merry men are we.

    Oh, give me, &c.

There's tempest in yon horned moon,
  And lightning in yon cloud—
And hark the music, mariners,
  The wind is piping loud;
The wind is piping loud, my boys!
  The lightning flashes free;
While the hollow oak our palace is,
  Our heritage the sea!

    Oh, give me, &c.

Will Watch.

'Twas one morn, when the wind from the northward blew keenly,
   While sullenly roar'd the big waves of the main,
A fam'd smuggler, Will Watch, kiss'd his Sue, then serenely
   Took helm, then to sea boldly steer'd out again.

Will had promis'd his Sue that his trip, if well ended,
   Should coil up his hopes, and he'd anchor on shore,
When his pockets were lin'd why his life should be mended,
   The laws he had broken he'd never break more.

His sea-boat was trim, made her port, took her lading,
   Then Will stood for home, reached her offing and cried,
This night, if I've luck, furls the sails of my trading.
   In dock I can lay, serve a friend too, beside.

Will lay-to till the night came on darksome and dreary,
   To crowd ev'ry sail on, he piped up each hand ;
But a signal soon spied, 'twas a signal uncheery,
   A signal that warn'd him to bear from the land.

The Philistines are out, cries Will, we'll take no heed on't,
   Attack'd, whose the man that would flinch from his gun?
Should my head be blown off I shall ne'er feel the need on't—
   We'll fight while we can, when we can't, boys, we'll run.

Thro' the haze of the night a bright flash now appearing,
   Oh, now! cries Will Watch, the Philistines bear down,
Bear a hand, my brave boys, ere we think about sheering—
   One broadside pour in, should we swing, boys, or drown.

And should I be popped off, you, my mates, left behind me ;
   Regard my last words—see 'em kindly obeyed ;
Let no stone mark the spot—and my friends do ye mind me,
   Near the beach is the spot where Will Watch would be laid.

Poor Will's yarn was spun out, for a bullet next minute
   Laid him low on the deck and never spoke more ;
His bold crew fought the brig while a shot remain'd in it,
   Then sheer'd and Will's hulk to his Susan they bore.

In the dead of the night his last wish was complied with,
  To few known his grave and to few known his end ;
He was borne to the earth by the crew that he died with,
  He'd the tears of his Susan and the prayers of each friend.

Near his grave dash the billows, the winds loudly bellow,
  Yon ash struck with lightning points out the cold bed,
Where Will Watch, the bold smuggler, that famed lawless fellow,
  Once fear'd, now forgot, sleeps in peace with the dead.

Yankee Sailors.

Yankee sailors have a knack,
  Haul away ! yeo ho, boys ;
Of pulling down a British Jack,
  'Gainst any odds, you know, boys.
Come three to one, right sure am I,
If we can't beat them sure we'll try
To make Columbia's colors fly,
  Haul away ! yeo ho, boys !

Yankee sailors, when at sea,
  Haul away ! yeo ho, boys !
Pipe all hands with merry glee,
  While aloft they go, boys !
And when with pretty girls on shore,
Their cash is gone, and not before,
They wisely go to sea for more,
  Haul away ! yeo ho, boys !

Yankee sailors love their soil,
  Haul away ! yeo ho, boys !
And for glory ne'er spare toil,
  But flog its foes, you know, boys !
Then while its standard owns a rag,
The world combined shall never brag
They made us strike the Yankee flag,
  Haul away ! yeo ho, boys !

Sailor's Tear.

He leaped into his boat as it lay upon the strand,
But, oh, his heart was far away with friends upon the land;
He thought of those he loved the best, a wife and infant dear,
And feeling filled the sailor's breast, the sailor's eye a tear!

They stood upon the far-off cliff, and waved a 'kerchief white,
And gazed upon his gallant bark, till she was out of sight,
The sailor cast a look behind, nor longer saw them near,
Then raised the canvas to his eye, and wiped away a tear!

Ere long o'er ocean's blue expanse his sturdy bark had sped,
The gallant sailor from her prow, descried a sail ahead,
And then he raised his mighty arm, his country's foes were near
Ay, then he raised his arm—but not to wipe away a tear.

The Sailor's Advice.

As you mean to set sail for the land of delight,
And in wedlock's soft hammock to swing every night,
If you hope that your voyage successful should prove,
Fill your sails with affection, your cabin with love.

Let your hearts, like the mainmast, be ever upright,
And the union you boast, like your tackle, be tight.
Of the shoals of indifference be sure to keep clear,
And the quicksands of jealousy never come near.

If husbands e'er hope to live peaceable lives,
They must reckon themselves, give the helm to their wives,
For the evener we go, boys, the better we sail,
On ship-board the helm is still ruled by the tail.

Then list to your pilot, my boys, and be wise;
If my precepts you scorn, and my maxims despise,
A brace of proud antlers your brows may adorn,
And a hundred to one but you double Cape Horn.

The Bonny Boat.

(JOANNA BAILEY.)

Oh, swiftly glides the bonny boat
  Just parted from the shore,
And to the fishers' chorus note
  Soft moves the dipping oar;
Their toils are borne with happy cheer;
  And ever may they speed,
That feeble age, and helpmate dear,
  And tender bairnies feed.

We cast our lines in Largo bay,
  Our nets are floating wide,
Our bonny boat with yielding sway,
  Rocks lightly on the tide;
And happy prove its daily lot,
  Upon the summer sea,
And blest on land our kindly cot,
  Where all our treasures be.

    We cast our lines in Largo bay, &c.

The mermaid on her rock may sing,
  The witch may weave her charm,
But water sprite nor eldritch thing
  The bonny boat can harm;
It safely bears its scaly store
  Through many a stormy gale,
While joyful shouts rise from the shore,
  Its homeward prow to hail.

    We cast our lines in Largo bay, &c.

Now, safe arrived on shore, we meet
   Our friends with happy cheer,
And with the fishers' chorus greet
   All those we hold most dear.
With happy cheer the echoing cove
   Repeats the chanted note,
As homeward to our cot we move
   Our bonny, bonny boat.

    We cast our lines in Largo bay, &c.

The Maltese Boat Song.

   See, brothers, see, how the night comes on,
Slowly sinks the setting sun;
Hark! how the solemn vesper's sound
Sweetly falls upon the ear;
   Then haste let us work till the daylight's o'er,
   And fold our nets as we row to the shore;
   Our toil of labor being o'er,
   How sweet the boatmen's welcome home,
   Home, home, home, the boatmen's welcome home,
   Sweet, oh sweet, the boatmen's welcome home.

See how the tints of daylight die,
Soon we'll hear the tender sigh;
For when the toil of labor's o'er,
We shall meet our friends on shore.
   Then haste, let us work till the daylight's o'er,
   And fold our nets as we row to the shore;
   For fame or gold howe'er we roam,
   No sound as sweet as welcome home.
   Home, home, home, the boatmen's welcome home,
   Sweet, oh sweet, the boatmen's welcome home.

    Then haste, &c.

Angel's Whisper.

A baby was sleeping,
Its mother was weeping,
For her husband was far o'er the wild raging sea,
And the tempest was swelling
Round the fisherman's dwelling,
And she cried, Dermot, darling, oh, come back to me.

Her beads while she number'd,
The baby still slumbered,
And smiled in her face as she bended her knee ;
Oh ! blessed be that warning,
My child, thy sleep adorning,
For I know that the angels are whispering to thee.
And while they are keeping
Bright watch o'er thy sleeping,
Ah, pray to them softly, my baby, with me ;
And say thou wouldst rather
They'd watch o'er thy father,
For I know that the angels are whispering to thee.

The dawn of the morning
Saw Dermot returning,
And the wife wept with joy, her babe's father to see,
And closely caressing
The child with a blessing,
Said, I knew that the angels were whispering to thee.

My Bounding Bark.

My bounding bark, I fly to thee,
  I'm wearied of the shore,
I long to hail the swelling sea,
  And wander free once more.
A sailor's life of reckless glee,
That only is the life for me.

I was not born for fashion's slave,
   Or the dull city's strife ;
Be mine the spirit-stirring wave,
   And roving sailor's life.
A life of freedom on the sea,
That only is the life for me.

I was not born for lighted halls,
   Or the gay revels round,
My music is where Ocean calls,
   And echoing rocks resound.
The wandering sailor's life of glee,
That only is the life for me.

The Sailor's Welcome Home.

When first at sea, the sailor lad
   So timid views the whitening billow,
And sighs for cot of mam or dad,
   Where flows the stream beneath the willow ;
But safe return'd, past dangers spurn'd,
   He laughs at ocean's threat'ning foam ;
Mam, sister, and he, all join with glee,
   To sing the sailor's welcome home.

When next at sea, the bolder youth
   No more ascends the mast with terror ;
Yet pensive, wishes Mary's truth
   May clear the rocks and shoals of error.
His voyage o'er, he comes ashore,
   And finds his heart could never roam ;
Then Poll and he get wed with glee,
   And sing the sailor's welcome home.

Lightly May the Boat Row.

Oh, calmly may the waves flow,
And lightly may the boat row,
And safe and swift the boat go,
   That my lad's in.
He plies the oar so tightly,
Moves in the dance so sprightly,
So gracefully and lightly,
   Oh, there are none like him!
Lightly may the boat row, the boat row, the boat row,
Lightly may the boat row that my lad's in.

I know he is true-hearted,
True-hearted, true-hearted;
He promised when we parted
   To come to me again.
Lightly may the boat row,
The boat row, the boat row,
Lightly may the boat row,
   That my lad's in.

    Lightly may the boat row, &c.

He wears a blue jacket,
Blue jacket, blue jacket,
He wears a blue jacket,
   And a dimple in his chin.
Lightly may the boat row,
The boat row, the boat row,
Lightly may the boat row,
   That my lad's in.

    Lightly may the boat row, &c.

The Wonderful Whale.

About a great Sea Snake you've heard,
    In a rare, astounding tale ;
So now I'll tell you what occurr'd,
    With a thumping South Sea Whale,
    With a monstrous South Sea Whale.
'Twas in the Autumn of the year
    We left the river's mouth,
And with a spread of sail did steer
    Towards the chilly South.

We reach'd our port then by degrees,
    And weather'd many a gale ;
When all at once our captain sees
    A thumping great big whale.
It crawl'd along like any snail,
    In a scorching sun at noon ;
Until they sent into its tail
    A jolly sharp harpoon.

Right mad with pain it quickly turn'd,
    And flew at harpoon Jack ;
But he its malice coolly spurn'd,
    By sticking at its back.
It rushed on, wounded fore and aft,
    Determin'd none to spare ;
Then put its tail beneath their craft,
    And threw 'em in the air.

By good luck, Jack, with oar in hand,
    Soon got upon the boat ;
And there he trembling did stand,
    This sad reverse to note.
The whale enraged then flew at Jack,
    While he for aid did bawl,
With a gaping mouth, and in a crack,
    It swallow'd him, boat and all.

Like Jonah in the whale's inside,
  Poor Jack was safely stow'd,
And when he came to himself, he cried,
  "I'm in it, now, I'm blow'd,
But I'll not sink on sight of rocks,
  Sours add but to the gripe;"
So out he lugged his backey box,
  And lighted up his pipe.

As Jack his cloud blew in the dark,
  The smoke grew pretty thick,
The whale, unused to such a lark,
  Soon turn'd uncommon sick.
This brought a thought into its sconce,
  To force Jack from below;
But Jack, who'd passed his teeth clear once
  Held fast, and cried, "No go."

The whale now grew so very ill,
  With pain it fairly sigh'd;
And though 'twas much against his will,
  Soon gave it up, and died.
Jack cut a hole then through its side,
  And quick put out his oar;
And having then a flowing tide,
  Safe rowed himself ashore.

Now Jack, when he the sand did reach,
  Ashore jump'd with a smile!
He drew the whale upon the beach,
  And his carcass sold for oil.
The truth our ship's crew don't deny,
  But tell it with a grin;
I only say, if it's all a lie
  We're nicely taken in.

All's Well.

(THOMAS DIBDIN.)

Deserted by the waning moon,
When skies proclaim night's cheerless noon,
On tower, or fort, or tented ground,
The sentry walks his lonely round,
And should a footstep haply stray
Where caution marks the guarded way,
    "Who goes there? Stranger quickly tell!
    A friend"—the word—"Good night—All's well!"

Or sailing on the midnight deep,
While weary messmates soundly sleep,
The careful watch patrols the deck
To guard the ship from foe or wreck;
And while his thoughts oft homeward veer,
Some well-known voice salutes his ear:
    "What cheer! oh, brother! quickly tell!
    Above! below! Good night! All's well!"

Harry Bluff.

When a boy Harry Bluff left his friends and his home
And his dear native land o'er the ocean to roam;
Like a sappling he sprung, he was fair to the view,
He was a true Yankee oak, boys, the older he grew;
Tho' his body was weak and his hands they were soft,
When the signal was given he the first went aloft;
The veterans all cried, "He'll one day lead the van,"
For tho' rated a boy, he'd the soul of a man,
    And the heart of a true Yankee sailor.

When to manhood promoted and burning for fame,
Still in peace or in war, Harry Bluff was the same,
So true to his love, and in battle so brave,
The myrtle and laurel entwin'd o'er his grave,
For his country he fell, when by victory crown'd
The flag shot away, fell in tatters around,
The foe thought he'd struck, but he sung out " Avast ! "
And Columbia's colors he nailed to the mast,
    And he died like a true Yankee sailor.

My Trim-Built Wherry.

(DIBDIN.)

Then farewell, my trim-built wherry—
  Oars, and coat, and badge farewell !
Never more at Chelsea ferry
  Shall your Thomas take a spell.

But to hope and peace a stranger,
  In the battle's heat I'll go,
Where expos'd to every danger,
  Some friendly ball shall lay me low.

Then mayhap, when homeward steering
  With the news my messmates come,
Even you the story hearing,
  With a sigh may cry — poor Tom !

Bay of Biscay, O.

(ANDREW CHERRY.)

Loud roared the dreadful thunder,
   The rain in deluge showers,
The clouds were rent asunder
   By lightning's vivid powers,
The night both drear and dark,
Our poor devoted bark,
Till next day there she lay
In the Bay of Biscay, O.

Now dashed upon the billow,
   Our op'ning timbers creak;
Each fears a watery pillow,
   None stop the dreadful leak,
To cling to slippery shrouds,
Each breathless seaman crowds,
As she lay till next day
In the Bay of Biscay, O.

At length the wish'd for morrow
   Broke through the hazy sky;
Absorb'd in silent sorrow,
   Each heaved a bitter sigh.
The dismal wreck to view
Struck horror to the crew,
As she lay, on that day,
In the Bay of Biscay, O.

Her yielding timbers sever,
   Her pitchy seams are rent,
When Heaven, all bounteous ever
   Its boundless mercy sent.
A sail in sight appears,
We hail her with three cheers;
Now we sail with the gale.
From the Bay of Biscay, O.

Far O'er the Deep Blue Sea.

The moon is beaming brightly, love,
    Upon the deep blue sea ;
A trusty crew is waiting near,
    For thee, dear girl, for thee ;
Then leave thy downy couch, my love,
    And with thy sailor flee,
His gallant bark shall bear thee safe
    Far o'er the deep blue sea :—

    Far—o'er the deep blue sea ;
    Far o'er th' deep, th' deep blue sea.

The storm-bird sleeps upon the rocks,
    No angry surges roar ;
No sound disturbs the tranquil deep,
    Not e'en the dipping oar ;
No watchful eye is on thee now,
    Come, dearest, hie with me,
And cheer a darling sailor's love
    Far o'er the deep blue sea.

    Far o'er, &c.

She comes, she comes, with trembling steps,
    Oh ! happy shall we be,
When landed safe on other shores,
    From every danger free ;
Now speed ye on my gallant bark,
    Our hopes are all in thee,
Swift bear us to our peaceful home,
    Far o'er the deep blue sea.

    Far o'er, &c.

The Lighthouse.

(MOORE.)

The scene was more beautiful far to my eye,
    Than if day in its pride had arrayed it ;
The land breeze blew mild and the azure arch'd sky
    Looked pure as the spirit that made it ;
The murmur arose as I silently gazed
    On the shadowy wave's playful motion,
From the dim distant isle till the beacon-fire blaz'd,
    Like a star in the midst of the ocean.

No longer the joy of the sailor boy's breast,
    Was heard in his wildly breathed numbers,
The sea-bird hath flown to her wave-girdled nest,
    The fisherman sunk to his slumbers ;
One moment I looked from the hill's gentle slope—
    All hush'd was the billows' commotion—
And methought that the beacon look'd lovely as hope,
    That star of life's tremulous ocean.

The time is long past, and the scene is afar ;
    Yet when my head rests on its pillow,
Will memory sometimes rekindle the star
    That blazed on the breast of the billow.
In life's closing hour, when the trembling soul flies,
    And death stills the heart's last emotion ;
O ! then may the seraph of mercy arise
    Like a star in eternity's ocean.

The Canadian Boat Song.

(MOORE.)

Faintly as tolls the evening chime,
Our voices keep tune, and our oars keep time,
Soon as the woods on shore look dim,
We'll sing at St. Ann's our parting hymn.
    Row, brothers, row, the stream runs fast,
    The rapids are near, and the daylight's past.

Why should we yet our sails unfurl?
There is not a breath, the blue waves to curl;
But when the wind blows from off the shore,
Oh, sweetly we'll rest our weary oar.

   Blow, breezes, blow, &c.

Utaw's tide! this trembling moon
Shall see us float o'er thy surges soon;
Saint of this green isle! hear our prayer,
Grant us cool heavens and favoring air.

   Blow, breezes, blow, &c.

Captain John Paul Jones' Victory.

Over the British frigate *Serapis*, and *Countess of Scarborough* sloop-of-war, during the American Revolution.

(September 23d, 1779.)

An American frigate—a frigate of fame,
With guns mounted forty, *Good Man Richard* by name,
Sailed to cruise in the channels of old England,
With a valiant commander, Paul Jones was the man.

He had not cruised long, before he espies
A large forty-four, and a twenty likewise;
Well manned with bold seamen, well laid in with stores,
In consort to drive us from old England's shores.

About twelve at noon, Percy came alongside,
With a loud-speaking trumpet, "Whence came you?" he cried;
"Return me an answer—I hailed you before,
Or if you do not, a broadside I'll pour."

Paul Jones then said to his men, every one,
"Let every true seaman stand firm to his gun ;
We'll receive a broadside from this Englishman,
And like true Yankee sailors return it again."

The contest was bloody, both decks ran with gore,
And the sea seemed to blaze while the cannon did roar ;
"Fight on, my brave boys," then Paul Jones he cried,
And soon we'll humble this bold Englishman's pride.

"Stand firm to your quarters—your duty don't shun,
The first one that shrinks, through the body I'll run ;
Though their force is superior, yet they shall know,
What true brave American seamen can do."

We fought them eight glasses, eight glasses so hot,
Till seventy bold seamen lay dead on the spot ;
And ninety brave seamen lay stretched in their gore,
While the pieces of cannon most fiercely did roar.

Our gunner in great fright to Captain Jones came,
"We gain water quite fast and our side's in a flame,"
Then Paul Jones he said in the height of his pride,
"If we cannot do better, boys, sink alongside."

The *Alliance* bore down, while the *Richard* did rake,
Which caused the bold heart of poor Percy to ache ;
Our shot flew so hot that they could not stand us long,
And the undaunted union of Britain came down.

To us they did strike and their colors haul down ;
The fame of Paul Jones to the world shall be known,
His name shall be ranked with the gallant and the brave,
Who fought like a hero our Freedom to save.

Now all valiant seamen, where'er you may be,
Who hear of this combat that's fought on the sea,
May you all do like them, when called to the same,
And your names be enrolled on the pages of fame.

Your country will boast of her sons that are brave,
And to you she will look, her from dangers to save,
She'll call you dear sons, in her annals you'll shine,
And the brows of the brave shall green laurels entwine.

So now, my brave boys, have we taken a prize—
A large forty-four and a twenty likewise,
Then God bless the mother whose doom is to weep
The loss of her sons in the ocean so deep.

Wilt Thou Tempt the Waves with Me?

Wilt thou tempt the waves with me,
   When the moon is high and bright,
And the ocean seems to be
   A pillow for her light?

I will tempt the waves with thee,
   When the moon is high and bright,
And the ocean seems to be
   A pillow for her light.

Stars will shine above us cheerily,
   As we glide along,
Whilst the rippling waters echo merrily
   To the mariner's song.

Wilt thou wander through the dells,
   Where our bower of beauty stands,
And the little silver bells
   Are rung by fairy hands?

I will wander through the dells,
   Where our bower of beauty stands,
And the little silver bells
   Are wrung by fairy hands.

Stars will shine above us cheerily,
   As we roam along,
Whilst the rippling waters echo merrily
   To the mariner's song.

The Gallant Tar to His Flag.

Float, beautiful flag, tho' the war cry is o'er,
    May thy stars and thy stripes ever wave;
To save thee from insult still, still would I fight,
    And e'en seek for a warrior's grave.

Beneath the great eagle with pinions spread wide,
    Have I cherished America's fame;
I fought not for glory, but fought for our rights,
    For I pride in my country's bright name.

America—e'en at the name our foes stand;
    We are born to be happy and free,
We drove our invaders away from our shores,
    And from tyrants we won liberty.

Wave on, stars and stripes, tho' our enemies boast,
    Of their nation we will not complain,
They may sail with the breeze, and plough the deep seas,
    But they cannot enslave us again.

Tho' we fall in our battles, we die for our land,
    With the hope that our country is blest,
With the sons of Columbia we mingle again,
    And sleep there where the warriors rest.

Then who would not die for the flag of the free
    Which will honor the tar's humble grave?
To save it from insult still, still would I fight;
    May thy stars and thy stripes ever wave.

Ply the Oar, Brother.

Ply the oar, brother, and speed the boat,
Swift o'er the glittering waves we float ;
Then home as swiftly we'll haste again,
Loaded with wealth of the plundered main.

   Pull away, pull away,
    Row, boys, row,
   A long pull, and a strong pull,
    And off we go.

Hark ! hark ! as the neighboring convent bell,
Throws o'er the waves its vesper swell,
Sullen its boom from shore to shore,
Blending its chime to the dash of the oar,
   Boom, boom—dash, dash !

   Pull away, &c.

The Mariner's Grave.

I remember the night was stormy and wet,
  And dismally dash'd the dark wave,
   While the rain and the sleet,
   Cold and heavily beat,
As we stood by the new-made grave.

I remember 'twas down in a darksome dale,
  And near to a dreary cave,
   Where the wild winds wail,
   Round the wanderer pale,
That I saw the Mariner's grave.

I remember how slowly the bearers trod,
  And how sad was the look they gave,
    As they rested their load
    Near its last abode,
  And gazed on the Mariner's grave.

I remember no sound did the silence break,
  As the corpse to the earth they gave,
    Save the night-bird's shriek,
    And the coffin's creak,
  As it sunk in the Mariner's grave.

I remember a tear that slowly slid
  Down the cheek of a messmate brave,
    It fell on the lid,
    And soon was hid,
  For closed was the Mariner's grave.

Now o'er his lone bed the brier creeps,
  And the wild flow'rs mournfully wave;
    And the willow weeps,
    And the moonbeams sleep,
  On the Mariner's silent grave.

Bessy, the Sailor's Bride.

Poor Bessy was a sailor's bride,
  And he was off to sea,
Their only child was by her side,
  And who so sad as she?

Forget me not, forget me not,
  When you are far from me,
And whatsoe'er poor Bessy's lot,
  She will remember thee.

A twelvemonth scarce had passed away,
  As it was told to me,
When Willy with a gladsome heart
  Came home again from sea.

He bounded up the craggy path
  And sought his cottage door,
But his poor wife and lovely child,
  Poor Willy saw no more.

"Forget me not, forget me not,"
  The words rung in his ear,
He asked the neighbors one by one,
  Each answer'd with a tear.

They pointed to the old churchyard,
  And there his youthful bride,
With the pretty child he loved so well,
  Were resting side by side.

Hurrah! I'm Off to Sea.

Away, away, I may not stand
  Where flowers and foliage be,
This dull small quiet spot of land,
  Is all too tame for me.
Three times I've travers'd round the world,
  Within your frigate free;
Again her canvas is unfurl'd,
  Hurrah! I'm off to sea.

Oh! who on one bright spot could dwell,
  Tho' all around were gay,
To see beneath joy's fairy spell
  That brightness wear away.
The birds that hover in the air
  Are happier far than we;
I'd something of their freedom share,
  Hurrah! I'm off to sea.

A thought—a cheering word—a sigh,
　　For friends and kindred here ;
A fervent wish—a fond good-bye,
　　For one more lov'd and dear ;
A shout for all that gallant crew,
　　Who plough the main with me ;
A parting look—a last adieu !
　　Hurrah ; I'm off to sea.

Deep, Deep Sea.

Oh, come with me, my love,
　　And our fairy home shall be,
Where the water spirits rove,
　　In the deep, deep sea.

There are jewels rich and rare,
　　In the cavern of the deep,
And to braid thy raven hair,
　　There the pearly treasures sleep.

In a tiny man-of-war,
　　Thou shalt stem the ocean tide,
Or in a crystal car
　　Sit a queen in all her pride.

Ah ! believe that love may dwell,
　　Where the coral branches twine,
And that every wreathed shell,
　　Breathes a tune as soft as thine.

Hope as fond as thou wilt prove,
　　Truth as bright as e'er was told,
Hearts as fond as those above,
　　Dwell under the water cold.

Gallant Tom.

(DIBDIN.)

It blew great guns, when gallant Tom
    Was taking in a sail,
And squalls came on in sight of home
    That strengthen'd to a gale ;
Broad sheets of vivid lightning glar'd
    Reflected by the main,
And even gallant Tom despair'd
    To see his love again.

The storm came on, each rag aboard
    Was into tatters rent,
The rain thro' every crevice pour'd,
    All fear'd the dread event ;
The pumps were chok'd, their awful doom,
    Seem'd sure at every strain,
Each tar despair'd, e'en gallant Tom,
    To see his love again.

The leak was stopp'd, the winds grew dull,
    The billows ceas'd to roar ;
And the torn ship, almost a hull,
    In safety reach'd the shore.
Crowds ran to see the wondrous sight,
    The storm had rag'd in vain ;
And gallant Tom, with true delight,
    Beheld his love again.

The Lad in the Jacket of Blue.

My love is a sailor and ploughs the salt seas,
    He's far from his country away,
But his heart is at home, for I know that his thoughts
    Are with Susan wherever he stray.

When the loud billows roar and the thunder is heard,
    While the gold-gleaming lightning I view,
Then I mingle a prayer with a sigh and a tear
    For the Lad in the Jacket of Blue.

Bright cherub that watches the life of a tar,
    Ah, guide home my William again,
For his ship o'er the cliff as I see him descend,
    I shall weep, but no, not in pain.

Then we'll dance on the beach, while the village bells ring,
    To welcome the brave and the true;
And a bride I'll become, yes, next Sunday, in church,
    To the Lad in the Jacket of Blue.

The Sailor's Consolation.

(WM. PITT.)

One night came on a hurricane,
    The sea was mountains rolling,
When Barney Buntline turn'd his quid,
    And said to Billy Bowling,
"A strong nor-wester's blowing, Bill,
    Hark! don't you near it roar now?
Lord, help them, how I pity's all
    Unhappy folks on shore now.

"Foolhardy chaps who live in town,
    What dangers they are all in,
E'en now are quaking in their beds
    For fear the roof should fall in;
Poor creatures, how they envies us,
    And wishes (I've a notion,)
For our good luck in such a storm,
    To be upon the ocean.

"But as for them who're out all day,
  On business from their houses,
And late at night are coming home
  To cheer their babes and spouses,
While you and I, Bill, on the deck
  Are comfortably lying,
My eyes! what tiles and chimney pots
  About their heads are flying.

"And often have we seamen heard
  How men are killed and undone,
By overturns of carriages,
  And thieves and fires in London.
We know what risks all landsmen run,
  From noblemen to tailors,
Then Bill, let us thank Providence,
  That you and I are sailors."

O Pilot, 'tis a Fearful Night.

(THOMAS HAYNES BAYLY.)

"O Pilot, 'tis a fearful night,
  There's danger on the deep;
I'll come and pace the deck with thee,
  I do not dare to sleep."
"Go down," the sailor cried, "go down,
  This is no place for thee;
Fear not, but trust in Providence,
  Wherever thou may'st be."
    "Fear not, but trust in Providence,
    Wherever thou may'st be."

"Ah, pilot, dangers often met
  We all are apt to slight;
And thou hast known these raging waves
  But to subdue their might."
"It is not apathy," he cried,
  "That gives this strength to me—
Fear not, but trust in Providence,
  Wherever thou may'st be.

"On such a night the sea engulfed
  My father's lifeless form;
My only brother's boat went down
  In just so wild a storm;
And such, perhaps, may be my fate,
  But still I say to thee,
Fear not, but trust in Providence,
  Wherever thou may'st be."

The Mariner.

Idle, as though a painted ocean,
  Listlessly mirrored a pictured boat,
Stranger to slightest thought of motion,
  Languidly calmed, a bark doth float.
Mariner, view heaven's spangled plain,
Mariner, view heaven's spangled plain,
Watching o'er thy dream, its myriad eye-stars reign.

Mariner, while thou liest sleeping,
  Whispers are heard in the distant north;
On the prophetic storm-cloud creeping,
  Signs that the boist'rous blast should forth,
Thunder may roll and lightning flame,
Thunder may roll and lightning flame,
God is watching ever o'er thee, still the same.

Hushed is the tempest; keep thy pillow,
  Zephyr breathes mildly the waters o'er,
Wafting thee safely through the billow,
  Showing at dawn the home-blest shore,
Love, thy returning kiss doth wait,
Love, thy returning kiss doth wait,
Kneel, and loudly praise such kind protecting fate.

Sailor Boy.

Sailor boy, sailor boy, sleep my sweet fellow ;
Sailor boy, sailor boy, sleep my sweet fellow,
   O'er your wreck'd vessel tho' thunderbolts roll,
Wild through the ocean wave loud the winds bellow,
   Calm be your bosom, for pure is your soul.
Hush a by, hush a by, poor sailor boy,
Let not the tempest your slumber destroy,
No terrors of conscience your bosom annoy,
Then hush a by, hush a by, poor sailor boy.

      Hush a by, &c.

Sailor boy, sailor boy, danger not bringing,
Sailor boy, sailor boy, danger not bringing,
   Home to your tho'ts crimes committed before,
Toss'd on rough seas, in a narrow cot swinging,
   Safer you sleep than a villain on shore.
Hush a by, hush a by, poor sailor boy,
Let not the tempest your slumber destroy,
No terrors of conscience your bosom annoy,
Then hush a by, hush a by, poor sailor boy.

      Hush a by, &c.

The Storm.

(GEORGE ALEXANDER STEVENS. Died 1784.)

   Cease, rude Boreas, blustering railer,
     List, ye landsmen, all to me,
   Messmates, hear a brother sailor
     Sing the danger of the sea ;
   From bounding billows first in motion,
     When the distant whirlwinds rise,
   To the tempest-troubled ocean,
     Where the seas contend with skies.

Hark! the boatswain hoarsely bawling
　By topsail sheets and halyards stand—
Down top-gallants quick be hauling—
　Down your staysails, hand, boys, hand;
Now it freshens, set the braces—
　Now the topsail sheets let go—
Luff, boys, luff, don't make wry faces—
　Up your topsails nimbly clew.

Now all you at home in safety,
　Shelter'd from the howling storm,
Tasting joys by Heaven vouchsafed ye,
　Of our state vain notions form.
Round us roars the tempest louder,
　Think what fear our minds enthralls;
Harder yet, it yet blows harder—
　Hark! again the boatswain calls!

The topsail yards point to the winds, boys,
　See all clear to reef each course—
Let the foresheet go—don't mind, boys,
　Though the weather should be worse.
Fore and aft the spritsail yard get—
　Reef the mizzen—see all clear—
Hands up, each preventer brace set,
　Man the foreyard—cheer, lads, cheer.

Now the dreadful thunder rolling,
　Peal on peal, contending, clash;
On our heads fierce rain is pouring,
　In our eyes blue lightnings flash;
One wide water all around us,
　All above us one black sky;
Different deaths at once surround us—
　Hark! what means that dreadful cry?

The foremast's gone! cries every tongue out,
  O'er the lee twelve feet 'bove deck;
A leak beneath the chest-tree's sprung out—
  Call all hands to clear the wreck.
Quick! the lanyards cut to pieces—
  Come, my hearts, be stout and bold!
Sound the well—the leak increases—
  Four feet water in the hold!

While o'er the ship wild waves are beating,
  We for wives or children mourn;
Alas! from hence there's no retreating—
  Alas! to them there's no return.
Still the leak is gaining on us,
  Both chain-pumps are choked below;
Heaven have mercy here upon us!
  For only that can save us now.

O'er the lee-beam is the land, boys—
  Let the guns o'erboard be thrown—
To the pumps come, every hand, boys—
  See! our mizzen-mast is gone,
The leak we've found—it cannot pour fast—
  We've lighten'd her a foot or more;
Up and rig a jury-foremast—
  She rights! she rights, boys! wear off shore.

Now, once more, peace around us beaming
  Since kind Heaven has saved our lives,
From our eyes joy's tears are streaming
  For our children and our wives:
Grateful hearts now beat in wonder
  To Him who thus prolongs our days—
Hush'd to rest the mighty thunder,
  Every voice bursts forth in praise.

The Phantom Ship.

'Twas midnight dark—
The seaman's bark
Swift o'er the waters bore him;
When, through the night,
He spied a light
Shoot o'er the wave before him.
"A sail! a sail!" he cries;
"She comes from the Indian shore,
And to-night shall be our prize,
With her freight of golden ore."
Sail on, sail on—
When morning shone
He saw the gold still clearer,
But though so fast
The waves he pass'd,
That boat seem'd never the nearer.

Bright daylight came,
And still the same
Rich bark before him floated;
While on the prize
His wishful eyes
Like any young lover's doted.
"More sail! more sail!" he cries,
While the wave o'ertops the mast,
And his bounding galley flies
Like an arrow before the blast.
Thus on, and on,
Till day was gone,
And the moon through heaven did hie her,
He swept the main,
But all in vain,
That boat seem'd never the nigher.

And many a day
To night gave way,
And many a morn succeeded,
While still his flight,
Through day and night,
That restless mariner speeded.

Who knows—who knows what seas
He is now careering o'er?
　Behind the eternal breeze,
And that mocking bark before!
　For oh! till sky
　And earth shall die,
And their death leave none to rue it,
　That boat must flee
　O'er the boundless sea,
And that ship in vain pursue it.

Jolly Sailor Bold.

It's when young men come home at night,
　They tell their girls fine tales
Of what they had been doing
　All day out in the fields.

The cutting of their grass or hay,
　It's all that they can do ;
Whilst we, like jolly hearts of gold,
　Do plough the ocean through.

The night's as dark as any pitch,
　When it begins to blow ;
The captain says, " My brave boys,
　Come up from below.

" Let every man on his deck stand
　Our gallant ship to guard ;
Aloft ! aloft ! " the captain cries ;
　" Pull down top-gallant yards ! "

When the wind and waves do meet,
　We are toss'd up and down ;
We lie close in a terror,
　For fear we would be drown'd.

"Hold up your hearts," the captain cries;
  "We'll see those girls again;
In spite of all our enemies,
  We will plough the raging main."

Thanks to kind Providence!
  We have got safe to shore;
We'll make the ale-house flourish,
  Ay! and the taverns roar.

We'll make the ale-house flourish,
  And spend our money free!
And when our money is all done,
  We'll boldly go to sea.

The Sea.

(BARRY CORNWALL.)

The sea! the sea! the open sea!
The blue, the fresh, the ever free!
Without a mark, without a bound,
It runneth the earth's wide regions round;
It plays with the clouds; it mocks the skies,
Or like a cradled creature lies.

I'm on the sea! I'm on the sea!
I am where I would ever be;
With the blue above, and the blue below,
And silence wheresoe'er I go;
If a storm should come and awake the deep,
What matter? I shall ride and sleep.

I love, oh! how I love to ride
On the fierce foaming, bursting tide,
When every mad wave drowns the moon,
Or whistles aloft his tempest tune,
And tells how goeth the world below,
And why the sou'west blasts do blow.

I never was on the dull tame shore,
But I lov'd the great sea more and more,
And backwards flew to her billowy breast,
Like a bird that seeketh its mother's nest ;
And a mother she was, and is to me ;
For I was born on the open sea !

The waves were white, and red the morn,
In the noisy hour when I was born ;
And the whale it whistled, the porpoise rolled,
And the dolphins bared their backs of gold,
And never was heard such an outcry wild
As welcomed to life the ocean's child.

I've lived since then, in calm and strife
Full fifty summers a sailor's life,
With health to spend and power to range
But never have sought nor sighed for change ;
And death, whenever he comes to me,
Shall come on the wild unbounded sea.

The Gondolier.

(MOORE.)

Row gently here, my gondolier ;
  So softly wake the tide,
That not an ear on earth may hear
  But hers to whom we glide.
Had heaven but tongues to speak as we,
  As starry eyes to see ;
Oh, think what tales 'twould have to tell
  Of wand'ring youths like me.
     Row gently, &c.

Now rest thee here, my gondolier;
  Hush, hush, for up I go—
To climb yon light belongs to night,
  Whilst thou keepeth watch below.
Ah! did we take for heaven above,
  But half such pains as we
Take day and night for woman's love,
  What angels we should be.

As Slow Our Ship.

(MOORE.)

As slow our ship her foamy track,
  Against the wind was cleaving,
Her trembling pennant still looked back
  To that dear isle 'twas leaving;
So doth we part from all we love,
  From all the links that bind us,
So turn our hearts, where'er we rove,
  To those we've left behind us.

When round the bowl of vanished years
  We talk, with joyous seeming,
With smiles that might as well be tears,
  So faint, so sad their beaming;
While mem'ry brings us back again
  Each early tie that twined us,
Oh! sweet's the cup that circles then
  To those we've left behind us.

And when in other climes we meet
  Some isle or vale enchanting,
Where all looks flowery, wild, and sweet,
  And naught but love is wanting;
We think how great had been our bliss,
  If heaven had but assigned us
To live and die in scenes like this,
  With some we've left behind us.

As travelers oft look back at eve,
  When eastward darkly going,
To gaze upon the light they leave
  Still faint behind them glowing:
So when the close of pleasure's day
  To gloom hath ne'er consigned us,
We turn to catch one fading ray
  Of joy that's left behind us.

A Life on the Ocean Wave.

(EPES SARGENT.)

A life on the ocean wave!
  A home on the rolling deep!
Where the scattered waters rave,
  And the winds their revels keep.
Like an eagle caged, I pine,
  On this dull, unchanging shore,
Oh! give me the flashing brine,
  The spray and the tempest's roar.

Once more on the deck I stand,
  Of my own swift-gliding craft;
Set sail—farewell to the land,
  The gale follows far abaft,
We shoot through the sparkling foam,
  Like an ocean bird set free,
Like the ocean bird, our home,
  We'll find far out on the sea.

The land is no longer in view,
  The clouds have begun to frown,
But with a stout vessel and crew,
  We'll say, let the storms come down.
And the song of our hearts shall be,
  While the winds and the waters rave,
A life on the heaving sea,
  A home on the bounding wave.

Sweet Poll, Adieu.

The gallant ship was under weigh,
　When up aloft Tom Halyard went,
To reef foretopsail, seeming gay,
　While cruel grief his bosom rent.
Think not a sniv'ling lubber he,
　From stem to stern no lad more true;
And helm a-weather or a-lee,
No tar was e'er so blythe as he,
　Till last he bade sweet Poll adieu.

An enemy appears in sight,
　The tars behold, with gladdened eye;
Tom breathes, ere they begin to fight,
　To heaven a prayer—for love, a sigh!
Yard-arm and yard-arm, now they go,
　While clouds of smoke obstruct the view,
Soon yielding, strikes the crippled foe,
But poor Tom Halyard is laid low,
　And sighs, in death, sweet Poll, adieu!

The news was like the thunder dread
　To Poll—Ah me! 'twas sad to see;
And from that hour her senses fled,
　A frantic wanderer is she.
Oft on the rocky beach she'll stray,
　Where fancy paints her love so true,
As, on that morning, forced away,
Which was to bring their wedding day,
　He faintly sighed—Sweet Poll, adieu.

The Sailor's Grave.

Our bark was out, far, far from land,
When the fairest of our gallant band,
Grew sadly pale, and waned away,
Like the twilight of an autumn day.

We watch'd him through long hours of pain,
But our cares were lost, our hopes were vain ;
Death struck, he gave no coward alarm,
For he smil'd as he died on a messmate's arm,
   For he smil'd as he died on a messmate's arm.

He had no costly winding sheet,
But we placed a round shot at his feet ;
And he slept in his hammock as safe and sound,
As a king in his lawn-shroud, marble bound.
We proudly deck'd his funeral vest,
With the stars and stripes above his breast ;
We gave him that as the badge of the brave,
And then he was fit for his sailor's grave.

Our voices broke, our hearts turn'd weak,
Hot tears were seen on the brownest cheek ;
And a quiver play'd on the lips of pride,
As we lower'd him down the ship's dark side.
A plunge—a splash—and our task was o'er,
The billows roll'd as they roll'd before ;
But many a rude prayer hallowed the wave,
That closed above the sailor's grave.

Faithful Poll.

(DIBDIN.)

Would'st thou know, my lad, why every tar
   Finds with his lass such cheer?
  'Tis all because he nobly goes.
   And braves each boisterous gale that blows,
To fetch from climates near and far,
   Her messes and her gear.
For this, around the world Jack sails,
   While love his bosom warms ;
For this, when safe and sound come back,
   Poll takes him to her arms.

Ere Poll can make the kettle boil
    For breakfast, out at sea,
  Two voyages long her Jack must sail,
  Encountering many a boisterous gale,
For the sugar to some western isle,
    To China for the tea.
To please her taste, thus faithful Jack
    Braves dangers and alarms,
While, grateful, safe and sound come back,
    Poll takes him to her arms.

Morocco shoes her Jack provides,
    To see her lightly tread;
  Her petticoat, of orient hue,
  And snow-white gown in India grew;
Her bosom Barcelona hides,
    Leghorn adorns her head.
Thus round the world sails faithful Jack,
    To deck his fair one's charms,
Thus, grateful, safe and sound come back,
    Poll takes him to her arms.

The Pilot.

When lightnings pierce the pitchy sky
And o'er the ocean's bosom fly,
While roaring waves each other 'whelm,
The hardy pilot takes the helm;
He puts to sea resolv'd to save,
Or perish in the briny wave.

Tho' signals of distress he hears,
And to the foundering vessel steers,
He loudly hails the exhausted crew,
Who cheer'd by him their toils renew,
And bless the pilot come to save,
Or perish in the briny wave.

They work the pumps with double force ;
He calmly points the helmsman's course,
His steady orders all obey,
And now the vessel on her way
Pursues, the pilot bent to save,
Or perish in the briny wave.

With anxious care, her course they keep,
She struggling rides the angry deep,
In smoother water soon she sails,
The crew huzza, then warmly hail,
The hardy pilot bent to save,
Or perish in the briny wave.

The Child of a Tar.

In a little blue garment all ragged and torn,
   With scarce any shoes to his feet ;
His head quite uncovered, a look all forlorn,
   And a cold stony step for his seat.
A boy cheerless sat, and as passengers pass'd,
   With a voice that might avarice bar,
Have pity, he cried, let your bounty be cast
   To a poor little child of a tar.

No mother I have, and no friend can I claim,
   Deserted and cheerless I roam ;
My father had fought for his country and fame,
   But alas! he may never come home.
Pinch'd by cold and by hunger, how hapless my state,
   Distress must all happiness mar,
Look down on my sorrow, and pity the fate
   Of a poor little child of a tar.

By cruelty drove from a neat rural cot,
  Where once with contentment we dwelt,
No friend to protect us, my poor mother's lot
  Alas! too severely she felt!
Bow'd down by misfortune, death made her his own,
  And snatched her to regions afar;
Distress'd and quite friendless, she left me to moan,
  A poor little child of a tar.

Thus plaintive he mourned, when a sailor that pass'd,
  Stopp'd a moment to give him relief,
He stretched forth his hand, and a look on him cast,
  A look full of wonder and grief.
What, my William, he faltered, my poor little boy,
  With wealth I'm returned from the war,
Thy sorrows shall cease, nor shall grief more annoy
  The poor little child of a tar.

The Light Bark.

Off! said the stranger, off, off, and away!
And away flew the light bark o'er the silvery bay,
We must reach ere to-morrow the far distant wave;
The billows we'll laugh at, the tempest we'll brave.

  Off, said the stranger, &c.

The young roving lovers their vows have been given,
Unsmiled o'er by mortals, yet hallowed in heaven;
She was Italy's daughter, I knew by her eye,
It wore the bright beam that illumines her sky.

  Off, said the stranger, &c.

And she has forsaken her palace and halls,
For the chill breeze and the light which falls
O'er the pure wave, from the heavens above,
And their guiding star was the bright star of love.

  Off, said the stranger, &c.

Blow High, Blow Low.

(DIBDIN.)

Blow high, blow low, let tempests tear
  The main-mast by the board ;
My heart with thoughts of thee, my dear,
  And love, well stored,
Shall brave all danger, scorn all fear,
  The roaring winds, the raging sea,
    In hopes on shore,
    To be once more
Safe moor'd with thee !

Aloft while mountains high we go,
  The whistling winds that scud along
And surges roaring from below,
    Shall my signal be
    To think on thee.

    Blow high, blow low, &c.

And on that night when all the crew
  The mem'ry of their former lives
O'er flowing cans of flip renew,
  And drink their sweethearts and their wives,
    I'll heave a sigh, and think on thee ;
    And as the ship rolls through the sea,
    The burthen of my song shall be—

    Blow high, blow low, &c.

While Up the Shrouds.

(DIBDIN.)

While up the shrouds the sailor goes,
    Or ventures on the yard,
The landsman, who no better knows,
    Believes his lot is hard ;

But Jack with smiles each danger meets,
 Casts anchor, heaves the log,
Trims all the sails, belays the sheets,
 And drinks his can of grog.

When mountains high the waves that swell
 The vessel rudely bear,
Now sinking in a hollow dell,
 Now quiv'ring in the air.
   Bold Jack, &c.

When waves 'gainst rocks and quicksands roar,
 You ne'er hear him repine,
Freezing on Greenland's icy shore,
 Or burning near the Line.
   Bold Jack, &c.

If to engage they give the word,
 To quarters all repair,
While splinter'd masts go by the board,
 And shot sing through the air.
   Bold Jack, &c.

The Busy Crew.

(DIBDIN.)

The busy crew their sails unbending,
 The ship in harbor safe arrived,
Jack Oakum all his perils ending,
 Had made the port where Kitty lived.

His rigging, no one dare attack it;
 Tight fore and aft, above, below;
Low-quarter'd shoes, check shirt, blue jacket,
 With trousers like the driven snow.

His honest heart with pleasure glowing,
  He flew like lightning to the side ;
Scarce had he been a boat's length rowing
  Before his Kitty he espied.

A flowing pennant gaily flutter'd
  From her neat-made hat of straw !
Red were her cheeks when first she utter'd
  It was "her sailor" that she saw.

And now the gazing crew surround her,
  While, secure from all alarms,
Swift as a ball from a nine-pounder,
  They dart into each other's arms.

Jack Ratlin.

(DIBDIN.)

Jack Ratlin was the ablest seaman,
  None like him could hand, reef, and steer,
No dangerous toil but he'd encounter
  With skill, and in contempt of fear.
In fight a lion; the battle ended,
  Meek as the bleating lamb he'd prove ;
Thus Jack had manners, courage, merit ;
  Yet did he sigh—and all for love.

The song, the jest, the flowing liquor,
  For none of these had Jack regard ;
He, while his messmates were carousing,
  High sitting on the pendant yard,
Would think upon his fair one's beauties,
  Swear never from such charms to rove ;
That truly he'd adore them living,
  And, dying, sigh—to end his love.

The same express the crew commanded
  Once more to view their native land,
Among the rest brought Jack some tidings,
  Would it had been his love's fair hand!
Oh, fate! her death defaced the letter;
  Instant his pulse forgot to move;
With quiv'ring lips, and eyes uplifted,
  He heaved a sigh—and died for love!

At Sea.

(DIBDIN.)

If tars of their money are lavish,
  I say, brother, take, take this from me,
'Tis because we are not muck-worms or slavish,
  Like lubbers who ne'er go to sea.
What's cunning and such quivication,
  And them sly manœuvres to we,
To be roguish is no valuation
  To hearties who plough the salt sea.

As for cheating, light weights, and short measures,
  And corruption and bribery, d'ye see,
They never embitter the pleasures
  Of good fellows who plough the salt sea.
You've ashore actions, writs, cessaries,
  And regiments of counsel to fee;
Jack knows not of such-like vagaries—
  We never trust lawyers at sea.

'Tis said that, with grog and our lasses,
  Because jolly sailors are free,
Our money we squander like asses,
  Which like horses we earn'd when at sea.
But let them say this, that, or t'other,
  In one thing they're forced to agree—
Honest hearts find a friend and a brother
  In each worthy that ploughs the salt sea.

Sweethearts and Wives.

(DIBDIN.)

'Twas Saturday night, the twinkling stars
    Shone on the rippling sea;
No duty called the jovial tars,
    The helm was lash'd a-lee;
The ample can adorn'd the board—
    Prepar'd to see it out,
Each gave the girl that he ador'd,
    And push'd the grog about.

Cried honest Tom, my Peg I'll toast,
    A frigate neat and trim,
All jolly Portsmouth's favorite boast;
    I'd venture life and limb—
Sail seven long years and ne'er see land,
    With dauntless heart and stout,
So tight a vessel to command;
    Then push the grog about.

I'll give, cried little Jack, my Poll,
    Sailing in comely state,
Top-ga'nt sails set, she is so tall,
    She looks like a first rate;
Ah! would she take her Jack in tow,
    A voyage for life throughout,
No better berth I'd wish to know;
    Then push the grog about.

I'll give, cried I, my charming Nan,
    Trim, handsome, neat, and tight;
What joy so fine a ship to man,
    She is my heart's delight!
So well she bears the storms of life,
    I'd sail the world throughout,
Brave ev'ry toil for such a wife:
    Then push the grog about.

Thus to describe Poll, Peg, or Nan,
  Each his best manner tried;
Till, summon'd by the empty can,
  They to their hammocks hied;
Yet still did they their vigils keep,
  Though the huge can was out,
For, in such visions, gentle sleep
  Still pushed the can about.

Saturday Night.

(DIBDIN.)

'Tis said we vent'rous die-hards when we leave the shore,
    Our friends should mourn,
    Lest we return
To bless their sight no more:
    But this is all a notion
    Bold Jack can't understand,
  Some die upon the ocean,
    And some upon the land.
      Then since 'tis clear
      Howe'er we steer,
  No man's life's under his command;
      Let tempests howl,
      And billows roll,
    And dangers press;
  Of these in spite, there are some joys
    Us jolly tars to bless,
  For Saturday night still comes, my boys,
    To drink to Poll and Bess.

One seaman hands the sails, another heaves the log,
   The purser swops
   Our pay for slops,
The landlord sells us grog :
  Then each man to his station
   To keep life's ship in trim :
  What argufies no ration ?
   The rest is all a whim.
     Cheerily, my hearts!
     Then play your parts,
  Boldly resolved to sink or swim ;
    The mighty surge
    May ruin urge,
   And dangers press ;
    Of these in spite, &c.

For all the world's just like the ropes aboard a ship,
   Each man's rigged out
   A vessel stout,
To take for life a trip,
  The shrouds, the stays, the braces,
   Are joys, and hopes, and fears ;
  The halyards, sheets, and traces,
   Still as each passion veers,
    And whim prevails,
    Directs the sails,
  As on the sea of life he steers,
    Then let the storm
    Heaven's face deform,
   And danger press ;
    Of these in spite, &c.

Yo, Heave, Ho !

(DIBDIN.)

The boatswain calls, the wind is fair,
The anchor heaving,
Our sweethearts leaving,
We to duty must repair,
 Where our stations well we know,

Cast off halyards from the cleets,
Stand by well, clear all the sheets;
Come, my boys,
Your handspikes poise,
And give one general huzza;
Yet sighing, as you pull away,
For the tears ashore that flow;
To the windlass let us go,
With yo, heave, ho!

The anchor coming now apeak,
Lest the ship, striving,
Be on it driving,
That we the tap'ring yards must seek,
   And back the foretop-sail well we know,
A pleasing duty! From aloft
We faintly see those charms, where oft,
When returning,
With passion burning,
We fondly gaze; those eyes that seem,
In parting, with big tears to stream.
But come! lest ours as fast should flow,
To the windlass once more go,
With yo, heave, ho!

Now the ship is under weigh,
The breeze so willing,
The canvas filling,
The press'd triangle cracks the stay,
   So taut to haul the sheet we know,
And now in trim we gaily sail,
The massy beam receives the gale;
While freed from duty,
To his beauty—
Left on the less'ning shore afar—
A fervent sigh heaves every tar;
To thank those tears for him that flow,
That from his true love he should go,
With yo, heave, ho!

True Yankee Sailor.

Jack dances and sings, and is always content,
  In his vows to his lass he'll ne'er fail her,
His anchor's a-trip when his money's all spent—
  And this is the life of a sailor.

Alert in his duty he readily flies,
  Where the winds the tired vessels are flinging,
Though sunk to the sea-gods, or toss'd to the skies,
  Still Jack is found working and singing.

'Longside of an enemy, boldly and brave,
  He'll with broadside on broadside regale her,
Yet he'll sigh to the soul o'er that enemy's grave,
  So noble's the mind of a sailor.

Let cannons roar loud, burst their sides let the bombs,
  Let the winds a dread hurricane rattle,
The rough and the smooth he takes as it comes,
  And laughs at the storm and the battle.

In a fostering power while Jack puts his trust,
  As fortune comes, smiling he'll hail her,
Resign'd still, and manly, since what must be must—
  And this is the mind of a sailor.

Though careless and headlong if danger should press,
  And rank'd 'mongst the free list of rovers,
Yet he'll melt into tears at a tale of distress,
  And prove the most constant of lovers.

To rancor unknown, to no passion a slave,
  Nor unmanly, nor mean, nor a railer,
He's as gentle as mercy, as fortitude brave—
  And this is a true Yankee sailor.

All's One to Jack.

(DIBDIN.)

Though mountains high the billows roll,
   And angry ocean's in a foam,
The sailor gaily slings the bowl,
   And thinks on her he left at home ;
Kind love his guardian spirit still,
His mind's made up, come what come will ;
Tempest may masts to splinters tear,
   Sails and rigging go to rack,
So she loves him he loves so dear,
      'Tis all one to Jack.

His friend in limbo should he find,
   His wife and children brought to shame,
To everything but kindness blind,
   Jack signs his ruin with his name.
Friendship the worthy motive still,
His mind's made up, come what come will ;
The time comes round, by hell-hounds press'd,
   Goods, clothes, and person go to rack ;
But, since he succor'd the distress'd
      'Tis all one to Jack.

Once more at sea prepared to fight,
   A friendly pledge round goes the can ;
And though large odds appear in sight,
   He meets the danger like a man.
Honor his guardian spirit still,
His mind's made up, come what come will ;
Like some fierce lion, see him go,
   Where horror grim marks the attack !
So he can save a drowning foe,
      'Tis all one to Jack.

And when at large (for tars and kings
   Must find in death a peaceful home)
The shot its sure commission brings,
   And of poor Jack the time is come—
Cheerful his duty to fulfill,
His mind's made up, come what come will;
The cannon's poised, from its fell jaws
   A fatal shot takes him aback;
But since he died in honor's cause
   'Twas all one to Jack.

The Sailor's Maxim.

(DIBDIN.)

Of us tars 'tis reported again and again,
That we sail round the world, yet know nothing of men;
And, if this assertion is made with the view
To prove sailors know nought of men's follies, 'tis true.
How should Jack practice treachery, disguise, or foul art,
In whose honest face you may read his fair heart!
Of that maxim still ready example to give,
Better death earn'd with honor than ignobly to live.

How can *he* wholesome truth's admonitions defy,
On whose manly brow never sat a foul lie?
Of the fair-born protector, how virtue offend?
To foe how be cruel? how ruin a friend?
If danger he risk in professional strife,
There his honor is safe, though he venture his life;
Of that maxim still ready example to give,
Better death earn'd with honor than ignobly to live.

But to put it at worst, from fair truth could he swerve,
And betray the kind friend he pretended to serve,
While snares laid with craft his fair honor trepan,
Man betray him to error, himself but a man;
Should repentance and shame to his aid come too late,
Wonder not if in battle he rush on his fate;
Of that maxim still ready example to give,
Better death earn'd with honor than ignobly to live.

The Heart of a True Yankee Sailor.

Would you know the ingredients that make up a tar?
   Take of courage and truth *quantum suff.;*
A soul, unsubdued by toil, tempest, and war;
   A temper quite easy—yet firm in a squall—
And a body of durable stuff;
   When Boreas, that blustering railer,
Blows great guns, that shivers stays, braces, and all—
   Save the heart of a true Yankee sailor!

Would you know what their hearts are composed of? Just take,
   All that friendship and love know of feeling
For sweetheart, or mate in distress, for whose sake
   He'd stand firm were the universe reeling!
Too proud to complain, be his lot e'er so low;
   Show him want! with his best he'll regale her;
Oppress him! and Jack's but a word and a blow
   From the heart of a true Yankee sailor!

About sympathy, Jack he knows nothing at all,
   Though he practices all its sweet duty;
Of purse-proud assurance whilst taking the wall,
   He yields it to age, worth, and beauty!
His ship is his glory—his captain's a king—
   Whose fiat ne'er finds him a failer?
Call ye that degradation? 'tis no such a thing
   In the heart of a true Yankee sailor!

Then mingle whate'er ye deem manly or mild,
   Tough, tender, keen, yet unsuspicious;
The nerve of a hero, the sigh of a child—
   All that nature esteems most delicious;
Fire the cauldron of Fancy, and put in all these,
   Envy's malice shall nothing avail her,
When she finds all on earth that can warm, charm, and please,
   In the heart of a true Yankee sailor!

Stand to Your Guns.

Stand to your guns, my hearts of oak,
Let not a word on board be spoke;
Victory is ours, 'mid fire and smoke;
  Be silent and be ready.
Ram home the guns and sponge them well,
Let us be sure the balls will tell;
The cannon's roar shall sound their knell;
  Be steady, boys, be steady.
Not yet, nor yet, nor yet;
Reserve your fire, I do desire.

Now the elements do rattle;
The gods amazed behold the battle.
  A broadside, my boys!
See the blood in purple tide
Trickle down her batter'd side.
Wing'd with fate the bullets fly,
Conquer, boys, or bravely die.
  She sinks, she sinks, she sinks, huzza!
To the bottom down she goes!

The Sailor's Bequest.

(Capt. WILLIS JOHNSON, R. N.)

The fight was o'er, and strew'd around
  Lay many a seaman brave,
And those who nobly died had found
  A deep unfathom'd grave.
One ling'ring lived, who vainly strove
  The manly tear to hide;
A pray'r he breath'd to Heav'n above,
  For her his promised bride.

'Twas poor Tom Ratline wounded lay,
  His life-blood ebbing fast;
On her he lov'd, far, far away.
  He felt he'd look'd his last.
"Shipmates," said he, "it is not dread
  Of death that fills my eye;
'Tis mem'ry's dream of joys, though fled,
  Which makes it sad to die.

"If our good prize should pay us well,
  Which I've no doubt she'll do,
Take all my share, and hark ye! tell
  The rhino out to Sue.
Dry her sweet eyes — salt tears they'll pour
  At poor Tom's fate," he cried;
"Say my last thought"— he could no more,
  But whisp'ring "Susan!" died.

The Mariner.

Hurra! along the foaming tide,
  With wild waves dashing round,
In furious speed I onward ride,
  And love the roaring sound.

Blow, blow, thou loud and fearful wind!
  Roll on, thou angry sea!
I'll drink to those I leave behind,
  I'll drink, Joanne, to thee!

Oh! who would tremble at the storm,
  Or, like the coward, weep?
I rather feel my bosom warm
  At every lengthen'd sweep.

The land is for the dastard mind—
  The deep, the deep, for me!
I'll drink to those I leave behind—
  I'll drink, Joanne, to thee!

Love, dearest maid, like mine shall ne'er
　In empty words depart ;
It still shall flourish, fresh and fair
　Within my faithful heart.

Yes! there's a power which dwells above
　That guards the brave and free ;
He sees, and will reward our love,
　So here's a health to thee !

Blow, blow, thou loud and fearful wind !
　Roll on, thou angry sea !
I'll drink to those I leave behind—
　I'll drink, Joanne, to thee !

The Heart Knows Only One.

The landsmen tell you those who roam
　O'er ocean's boundless tide,
On ev'ry shore can find a home,
　In ev'ry port a bride.
Heed not, sweet maid, their idle prate,
　They ne'er such feelings knew
As warm the heart of thy sailor-mate,
　Which beats alone for you.

What though, when storms our bark assail,
　The needle trembling veers,
When night adds horrors to the gale,
　And not a star appears ?—
True to the pole as I to thee,
　It faithful still will prove
An emblem, dear, of constancy,
　And of a sailor's love.

Then turn from what the landsmen say,
  Who would thy faith beguile;
They seize the time when we're away
  To practice every wile;
O'er beauty bright our looks may rove,
  We ne'er its influence shun,
But though the eye has many a love,
  The heart knows only one.

Life's Troubled Sea.

This life is a troubled sea,
Where, helm a-weather or a-lee,
The ship will neither stay nor wear,
But drives, of every rock in fear.

All seamanship in vain we try,
We cannot keep her steadily;
But just as fortune's wind may blow,
The vessel's tosticated to and fro;
Yet, come but love on board,
Our heart's with pleasure stored,
No storms can overwhelm;
  Still blows in vain
  The hurricane,
While love is at the helm.

Hurrah for the Sea.

Your poets may sing of the pleasures of home,
  Of the land and a bright sunny sky;
Give me the rough ocean with bosom of foam,
  And a bark, when in chase, that will fly;
Though aloft to the clouds on the billows we soar,
  And then sink to the valley below,

We danger defy, 'mid the hurricane's roar,
   And reck not, how hard it may blow !
Then hurrah for the sea, boys ! hurrah for the sea !
   The mariner's life is the life for me.

The dear ones we love, when our pockets are lined,
   Help to spend all our rhino on shore,
And when empty, "up anchor!" we're sure soon to find
   A prize that will furnish them more.
All friends we avoid as we roam o'er the wave ;
   The sail which we welcome's a foe ;
And should death heave us to, there's a ready-made grave,
   And down to the bottom we go !
Then hurrah for the sea, boys ! hurrah for the sea !
   A mariner's life is the life for me.

The Lighthouse.

Our sea-borne chimes eight bells have toll'd
   Far o'er the wat'ry waste ;
To distant ships their sound has roll'd ;
The canvas drips with night-dew cold ;
   The mid-hour watch is placed.
Look out ! look out, my trusty crew !
   Strain every anxious eye ;
Though spray and mist obscure the view,
   We know the land is nigh !

And spare ye not the plunging lead,
   As carefully we steer ;
What star shines o'er the lee cathead,
Which now gleams forth with lustre red,
   Now seems to disappear?
It is no star ! I see it now !
   It is the lighthouse beam,
Which from yon tall cliff's beetling brow
   Sheds forth its changeful gleam.

A sailor's thanks to those who tend,
  Its true though fitful light,
Who, like our guardian angels, lend
Their ceaseless vigils to befriend
  The wand'ring vessel's flight.
No strangers, now, the deep we roam !
  Shake out, shake out the reefs ; make sail ;
That lighthouse is the light of home,
  And hope breathes in the gale.

As still we coast the rugged steep,
  The lighthouse sheds its ray ;
But there's a love which does not sleep,
And hearts which watch as constant keep,
  When we are far away.
What transport in each breast will glow,
  When, with to-morrow's sun,
Our well-known signal-flags shall show
  The destin'd port we've won.

The Signal to Engage.

(DIBDIN.)

The signal to engage shall be
  A whistle and a halloa ;
Be one and all but firm, like me,
  And conquest soon will follow.

You, Gunnel, keep the helm in hand—
  Thus, thus, boys ! steady, steady,
Till right ahead you see the land,
  Then, soon as we are ready,
    The signal, &c.

Keep, boys, a good lookout, d'ye hear,
  'Tis for our country's honor ;
Just as you brought your lower tier
  Broadside to bear upon her,
    The signal, &c.

All hands then, lads, the ship to clear!
Load all your guns and mortars;
Silent as death th' attack prepare;
And when you're all at quarters,

    The signal, &c.

Foretop Morality.

(DIBDIN.)

Two real tars, whom duty call'd
    To watch in the foretop,
Thus one another overhaul'd,
    And took a cheering drop,
I say, Will Hatchway, cried Tom Tow,
    Of conduct what's your sort,
As through the voyage of life you go,
    To bring you safe to port?

Cried Will, you lubber, don't you know?
    Our passions close to reef,
To steer where honor points the prow,
    To hand a friend relief:
These anchors get but in your power,
    My life for't that's your sort,
The bower, the sheet, and the best bower,
    Shall bring you up in port.

Why then you're out, and there's an end,
    Tom cried out blunt and rough,
Be good, be honest, serve a friend,
    Be maxims well enough;
Who swabs his bows at other's woe,
    That tar's for me your sort;
His vessel right ahead shall go
    To find a joyful port.

Let storms of life upon me press,
    Misfortunes make me reel,
Why, dam'me, what's my own distress,
    For others let me feel.
Ay, ay, if bound with a fresh gale
    To heaven, this is your sort,
A handkerchief is the best wet sail
    To bring you safe to port.

The Wandering Sailor.

The wand'ring sailor ploughs the main
A competence in life to gain ;
Undaunted braves the stormy seas
To find, at last, content and ease ;
In hopes, when toil and danger's o'er
To anchor on his native shore.

When winds blow hard, and mountains roll,
And thunders shake from pole to pole,
Though dreadful waves surrounding foam,
Still flatt'ring fancy wafts him home ;
    In hopes, &c.

When round the bowl the jovial crew
The early scenes of youth renew,
Though each his fav'rite fair will boast
This is the universal toast :
" May we, when toil and danger's o'er,
Cast anchor on our native shore."

The Mid-Watch.

(R. B. SHERIDAN.)

When 'tis night, and the mid-watch is come,
    And chilling mists hang o'er the darken'd main,
Then sailors think of their far distant home,
    And of those friends they ne'er may see again.

    But when the fight's begun,
    Each serving at his gun,
Should any thought of them come o'er our mind,
  We think, should but the day be won,
    How 'twill cheer
    Their hearts to hear
That their old companion he was one!

Or, my lad, if you a mistress kind
 Have left on shore, some pretty girl and true,
Who many a night doth listen to the wind,
 And sighs to think how it may fare with you—
    O when the fight's begun,
    Each serving at his gun,
Should any thought of her come o'er your mind,
  Think, only should the day be won,
    How 'twill cheer
    Her heart to hear
That her own true sailor he was one!

The Hardy Sailor.

 The hardy sailor braves the ocean,
  Fearless of the roaring wind;
 Yet his heart with soft emotion
  Throbs to leave his love behind.

To dread of foreign foes a stranger,
 Though the youth may dauntless roam,
Alarming fears paint ev'ry danger
 In a rival left at home.
    The hardy sailor, &c.

Aloft the Sailor Looks Around.

From aloft the sailor looks around,
And hears below the murm'ring billows sound ;
Far off from home he counts another day,
While o'er the seas the vessel bears away !
    His courage wants no whet,
    But he springs the sail to set
With heart as fresh as rising breeze of May ;
    And caring nought,
    He turns his thought
To his lovely Sue or his charming Bet.

Now to heav'n the lofty topmast soars,
The stormy blast like dreadful thunder roars,
Now ocean's deepest gulfs appear below,
The curling surges foam, and down we go !
    When skies and seas are met,
    They his courage serve to whet ;
With a heart as fresh as rising breeze of May ;

    And dreading nought, &c.

Loose Every Sail to the Breeze.

1815.

Come, loose every sail to the breeze,
    The course of my vessel improve ;
I've done with the toils of the seas—
    Ye sailors, I'm bound to my love.

Since Emma is true as she's fair,
    My griefs I fling all to the wind ;
'Tis a pleasing return to my care,
    My mistress is constant and kind.

My sails are all fill'd to my dear;
   What tropic-bird swifter can move?
Who cruel shall hold his career
   That returns to the nest of his love?

Hoist every sail to the breeze;
   Come, shipmates, and join in the song;
Let's drink while the ship cuts the seas,
   To the gale that may drive her along.

Moorings.

(DIBDIN.)

I've heard, cried out one, that you tars tack and tack,
   And at sea what strange hardships befel you;
But I don't know what's moorings. What, don't you know? said Jack;
Man your ear-tackle then, and I tell you;
Suppose you'd a daughter quite beautiful grown,
   And in spite of her prayers and implorings,
Some scoundrel abused her, and you knock'd him down,
   Why, d'ye see, he'd be safe at his moorings.

In life's voyage should you trust a false friend with the helm,
   The top-lifts of his heart all akimbo,
A tempest of treachery your bark will o'erwhelm,
   And your moorings will soon be in limbo;
But if his heart's timbers bear up against pelf,
   And he's just in his reckoning and scorings,
He'll for you keep a look-out the same as himself,
   And you'll find in his friendship safe moorings.

If wedlock's your port, and your mate, true and kind,
　　In all weathers will stick to her duty,
A calm of contentment shall beam in your mind,
　　Safe moor'd in the haven of beauty ;
But if some frisky skiff, crank at every joint,
　　That listens to vows and adorings,
Shape your course how you will, still you'll make Cuckold's
　　　　Point,
　　To lay up a beacon at moorings.

A glutton's safe moor'd, head and stern, by the gout,
　　A drunkard's moor'd under the table,
In straws drowning men will Hope's anchor find out,
　　While a hair's a philosopher's cable ;
Thus mankind are a ship, life a boisterous main,
　　Of Fate's billows where all hear the roarings,
Where for one calm of pleasure we've ten storms of pain,
　　Till death brings us all to our moorings.

Anna, Anne, Nan, Nance, or Nancy.

(DIBDIN.)

My love's a vessel trim and gay,
　　Rigg'd out with truth and stored by honor ;
As through life's seas she cuts her way,
　　All eyes with rapture gaze upon her ;
Built every wondering heart to please—
　　The lucky shipwrights love and fancy ;
From stem to stern she moves with ease,
　　And at her launch they call'd her Nancy.

When bearing up against life's gales,
　　So well she stems the dangerous trouble,
I call her Anna—as she sails,
　　Her form's so grand, her air's so noble,
When o'er the trembling wave she flies,
　　That plays and sports as she advances,
Well said, my Nan ! I fondly cries,
　　As my full heart in concert dances.

In studding sails before life's breeze
  So sweetly gentle is her motion,
She's Anne—for as she moves with ease,
  She seems the queen of all the ocean,
But when on Sundays rigg'd in stays,
  Like beauty gay and light as fancy,
She wins my heart a thousand ways;
  I then delight to call her Nancy.

When laying on a tack so neat,
  The breeze her milk-white bosom filling,
She skims the yielding waves so fleet,
  I call her Nance, my bosom thrilling.
Thus is she precious to my heart,
  By whate'er name comes o'er my fancy.
Graceful or gay, grand, neat, or smart,
  Or Anna, Anne, Nan, Nance, or Nancy.

The Helmsman's Song.

(MOORE.)

When freshly blows the northern gale,
  And under courses snug we fly,
Or when light breezes swell the sail,
  And royals proudly sweep the sky;
'Longside the wheel, unwearied still
  I stand; and, as my watchful eye
Doth mark the needle's faithful thrill,
  I think of her I love, and cry,

    Port, my boy! port.

When calms delay, or breezes blow
  Right from the point we wish to steer;
When by the wind close-haul'd we go,
  And strive in vain the port to near,

I think 'tis thus the fates defer
  My bliss with one that's far away ;
And, while remembrance springs to her,
  I watch the sails, and sighing say,

    Thus, my boy ! thus.

But see, the wind draws kindly aft,
  All hands are up the yards to square,
And now the floating stu'nsails waft
  Our stately ship through waves and air.
Oh ! then I think that yet for me,
  Some breeze of fortune thus may spring,
Some breeze to waft me, love, to thee—
  And in that hope I smiling sing,

    Steady, boy ! So !

The Return of the Admiral.

(BARRY CORNWALL.—Bryan Waller Proctor.)

How gallantly, how merrily,
  We ride along the sea !
The morning is all sunshine,
  The wind is blowing free ;
The billows are all sparkling,
  And bounding in the light,
Like creatures in whose sunny veins
  The blood is running bright.
All nature knows our triumph,
  Strange birds about us sweep ;
Strange things come up to look at us,
  The masters of the deep ;
In our wake, like any servant,
  Follows even the bold shark,
Ah, proud must be our admiral
  Of such a bonny bark !

Proud, proud must be our admiral,
  (Though he is pale to-day,)
Of twice five hundred iron men,
  Who all his nod obey;
Who've fought for him and conquer'd,—
  Who've won, with sweat and gore,
Nobility! which he shall have
  Whene'er he touch the shore.
Oh! would I were an admiral,
  To order with a word;
To lose a dozen drops of blood,
  And straight rise up a lord;
I'd shout e'en to yon shark there,
  Who follows in our lee,
" Some day I'll make thee carry me
Like lightning through the sea."

The admiral grew paler,
  And paler as we flew,
Still talk'd he to his officers,
  And smiled upon his crew;
And he looked up at the heavens,
  And he looked down on the sea,
And at last he spied the creature,
  That kept following in our lee.
He shook—'twas but an instant;—
  For speedily the pride
Ran crimson to his heart,
  Till all chances he defied;
It threw boldness on his forehead;
  It gave firmness to his breath;
And he stood like some grim warrior,
  New risen up from death.

That night, a horrid whisper
  Fell on us where we lay;
And we knew our fine old admiral
  Was changing into clay;
And we heard the wash of waters,
  Though nothing could we see,

And a whistle and a plunge
  Among the billows in our lee!
Till dawn we watch'd the body,
  In its dead and ghastly sleep,
And next evening at sunset,
  It was launch'd into the deep!
And never from that moment,
  Save one shudder through the sea,
Saw we, or heard, the shark
  That had follow'd in our lee!

The Stormy Petrel.

(BARRY CORNWALL—Bryan W. Proctor.)

A thousand miles from land are we,
Tossing about on the roaring sea;
From billow to bounding billow cast,
Like fleecy snow on the stormy blast:
The sails are scattered abroad, like weeds;
The strong masts shake, like quivering reeds;
The mighty cables, and iron chains,
The hull, which all earthly strength disdains,
They strain and they crack, and hearts like stone
Their natural hard proud strength disown.

Up and down! Up and down!
From the base of the wave to the billows' crown,
And amidst the flashing and feathery foam
The stormy Petrel finds a home—
A home, if such a place may be
For her who lives on the wide, wide sea,
On the craggy ice, in the frozen air,
And only seeketh her rocky lair
To warm her young, and to teach them spring
At once o'er the waves on their stormy wing!

O'er the deep! O'er the deep!
Where the whale, and the shark, and the sword-fish sleep,
Outflying the blast and the driving rain,
The Petrel telleth her tale in vain;
For the mariner curseth the warning bird,
Who bringeth him news of the storms unheard!
Ah, thus does the prophet of good or ill,
Meet hate from the creatures he serveth still;
Yet he ne'er falters. So, Petrel, spring
Once more o'er the waves on thy stormy wing!

Serving in the Navy.

[Air: "Marching through Georgia."]

Oh! we are gay Apprentice boys,
    To the Navy we belong.
Though gathered from the city or
    The farm, we're young and strong.
And we can box the compass, reef
    And steer, or sing a song,
While we are serving in the Navy.

CHORUS.

Hurrah! hurrah! right jolly tars are we.
Hurrah! hurrah! our home the deep blue sea.
We'll serve our time in every clime,
    And cruise o'er every sea,
While we are serving in the Navy.

There's lots of fun before us, boys,
    Wherever we may go,
We'll flirt with the Kanaka girls—
    The maids of Cal-la-o.
We'll learn to dance the hula and
    The Zamacueca, too.
While we are serving in the Navy.

But, though bewitching sirens seek
  Our hearts with love to bind,
I'm sure we never will forget
  The girls we've left behind.
Though joys enchant and pleasures lure,
  Our love is theirs they'll find,
While we are serving in the Navy.

The honor of our flag we'll guard,
  The glorious stripes and stars,
Protect it with our lives if we're
  Involved in foreign wars.
We're ready for the battle and
  We do not fear the scars,
While we are serving in the Navy.

The Pillar of Glory.

(EDWIN C. HOLLAND, Charleston, S. C.)

Hail to the Heroes whose triumphs have brighten'd
  The darkness which shrouded America's name ;
Long shall their valor in battle that lighten'd
  Live in the brillant escutcheons of fame ;
    Dark where the torrents flow,
    And the rude tempests blow,
The stormy clad Spirit of Albion raves ;
    Long shall she mourn the day,
    When, in the vengeful fray,
Liberty walk'd like a God on the waves.

The ocean, ye chiefs, (the region of glory,
  Where Fortune has destin'd Columbia to reign)
Gleams with the halo and lustre of story,
  That curl round the wave as the scene of her fame ;
    There, on its raging tide,
    Shall her proud *Navy* ride,
The bulwark of freedom, protected by Heav'n ;
    There shall her haughty foe
    Bow to her prowess low,
There shall renown to her heroes be giv'n.

The Pillar of Glory, the sea that enlightens,
   Shall last till Eternity rocks on its base,
The splendor of Fame its waters that brightens,
   Shall light the footsteps of Time in his race;
     Wide o'er the stormy deep,
     Where the rude surges sweep,
Its lustre shall circle the brows of the brave;
     Honor shall give it light,
     Triumph shall keep it bright,
Long as in battle we meet on the wave.

Already the storm of contention has hurl'd
   From the grasp of Old England the *Trident of War*,
The beams of our *Stars* have illumin'd the world,
   Unfurl'd, our Standard beats proud in the air:
     Wild glares the eagle's eye,
     Swift as he cuts the sky,
Marking the wake where our heroes advance;
     Compass'd with rays of light,
     Hovers he o'er the fight;
Albion is heartless—and stoops to his glance.

Rise, Columbia, Brave and Free.

(EDWIN C. HOLLAND, Charleston, S. C.)

When Freedom first the triumph sung,
   That crush'd the pomp of Freedom's foes,
The harps of Heav'n responsive rung,
   As thus the choral numbers rose:

     Rise, Columbia! brave and free!
       Thy thunder, when in battle hurl'd,
     Shall rule the billows of the sea,
     And bid defiance to the world.

Supremely blest by Fate's decree,
  Thy hardy tars in battle brave,
Shall plume thy wings, and keep thee free,
  As in the motion of thy wave :
    Rise, Columbia ! &c.

The stars that in thy banner shine,
  Shall rain destruction on thy foes,
Yet light the brave of ev'ry clime
  To kindred friendship and repose :
    Rise, Columbia ! &c.

The storms that on thy surges rock,
  Around thy flag shall idly sweep,
Proof to the tempest's fiercest shock,
  Its stripes shall awe the vassal deep :
    Rise, Columbia ! &c.

Encircled with a flood of light,
  Thy eagle shall supremely rise,
Lead thee to victory in fight,
  And bear thy glory to the skies :
    Rise, Columbia ! &c.

Ye Sons of Columbia.

[Tune : " Hearts of Oak."]

Ye sons of Columbia, come let us rejoice
  In the bright course of glory our brave tars have run,
And in one mighty chorus, with one heart and voice,
  Pour the tribute of verse o'er the laurels they've won.
    Hearts of oak are our ships, souls of fire are our men,
      They always are ready,
      Steady, boys, steady,
    To fight and to conquer again and again.

Oh! long on our mountains the forests have stood,
   Through ages of peace, in the shade of neglect;
But the fiat of Heaven calls them down to the flood,
   Our shores to defend, and our rights to protect.
        Hearts of oak, &c.

And see while the nations of Europe have long,
   'Mid the conflicts of war, rear'd their pillars of fame,
We can boast of our heroes, whose claims are as strong,
   Whose achievements will give them as deathless a name.
        Hearts of oak, &c.

See Hull, Jones, Decatur, and Bainbridge now burn
   Brighter stars in our land than vain Britons can claim,
For while they beat the world, we beat them in our turn,
   And thus prostrate at once their proud *pillars of fame.*
        Hearts of oak, &c.

Behold too brave Lawrence, whose splendid career
   Gives another bright star to the sky of our fame,
Though remov'd from this world, his example shall rear
   Future heroes in war, "by the fame of his name."
        Hearts of oak, &c.

And see, too, young Burroughs, the seaman's delight,
   Bears another *fair* sprig pluck'd from Victory's brow,
Tho' 'twas bought by his life-blood that stream'd in the fight,
   Life 'gainst *honor* is naught, as our brave tars well know.
        Hearts of oak, &c.

But hark! while we sing, hear the trumpet of fame,
   With the glad notes of triumph, again our ears greet;
'Tis for Perry it swells, ever-glorious name,
   To whose matchless arm *struck a whole British fleet.*
        Hearts of oak, &c.

We've yet thousands besides of young sons of the wave,
  Who but wait for the call of their country to fly,
And to enter the lists, with the first of the brave,
  Who their honor insult, or their prowess defy.

      Hearts of oak, &c.

Then ye sons of Columbia, come let us rejoice,
  In the bright course of glory our country can boast,
And in one mighty chorus, with one heart and voice,
  While we drink to our tars, let this still be our *toast,*
    Hearts of oak are our ships, sons of fire are our men,
      They always are ready,
      Steady, boys, steady,
  For their country to fight, and to conquer again.

'Tis the Deed of the Brave.

Sung at the public dinner, given to Com. Perry, in Boston, May 11th, 1814.

(Written by MR. CHARLES SPRAGUE.)

[Tune: "Anacreon in Heaven."]

'Tis the deed of the BRAVE! sound the Pæan of praise,
  As here in festivity's glee we assemble;
Quaff the brisk mantling bowl, and the choral strain raise,
  To the CHIEF who bade *ocean's invincibles* tremble.
    Oh! long by each tongue
    Shall *his* prowess be sung,
Whose time-lasting deeds o'er the lake-wave have rung.

      CHORUS.

  Enriched by humanity's balm in his heart,
  Round his brow the young laurels sweet odors impart.

Lov'd, natal COLUMBIA! though rocky thy shores,
  Yet thy soil is prolific in HEROES and SAGES;
Though the surge sweeps thy cliffs where the storm-spirit roars,
  Here the OAK-PLANT of FREEDOM shall flourish through ages!
      On blood-crimson'd soil,
      Thy brave YEOMANRY toil,
And on hill-tops they culture, invasion will foil.

CHORUS.

  And long shall thy TARS move in pride o'er the deep,
  Where thy star-studded banners in victory sweep.

Oh! long in the fancy-wrought Heaven of Fame,
  Thy HEROES, a starry-gay cluster shall brighten;
There the ne'er-waning orb of each glory-girt name,
  Through the vapors of time shall eternally lighten.
      In our cloud-curtain'd way,
      They emit a bright ray,
    To lead us to conquest, to honor and day.

CHORUS.

  Then, freemen, march onward! their beams shall illume
  Our pathway to glory, and shield us from gloom.

Scorn shadow his path, to the dust bid him bend,
  Who the rank-springing seeds of submission would scatter;
Let the *Nazarite's* fate in full vengeance descend
  On the wretch who the pillars of freedom would shatter,
      Oh! here let us swear,
      That the fabric so fair,
By our HEROES uprear'd, shall be shielded with care:

CHORUS.

  Coeval to live, with the hills of the West,
  Till time's final shock give the nations to rest.

Now peace to the BRAVE, who in battle have died,—
  Their deeds with the chaplet of fame have enwreath'd them,
Let the children of minstrelsy chant them with pride,
  And prosperity rival th' examples bequeath'd them.
      When the oaks of the vale
      Are unmoor'd to the gale,
Each friend to protect, and each foe to assail.

        CHORUS.

  Future PERRYS shall rise, and the world shall behold
  NEW deeds and NEW HEROES to page with the OLD.

The Hero of Erie.

(Written by JOHN PEIRPONT, Esq.)

[Tune : "In the Downhill of Life."]

O'er the mountains the sun of our fame was declining,
  And on Tethys's billowy breast
The cold orb had repos'd, all his splendor resigning,
  Bedimm'd by the mists of the West.
The prospect that rose to the patriot's sight
  Was cheerless, and hopeless and dreary :—
But a bolt burst the cloud, and illumin'd the night
  That envelop'd the waters of Erie—
The gray god of the Lake left his palace of coral,
  And moving sublime o'er the wave,

From the bank where it bloom'd pluck'd a chaplet of laurel,
  And the garland to Victory gave.
By the goddess 'twas held o'er each thundering deck,
  Till with doubts grown distracted and weary ;—
And when each gun was silent, each vessel a wreck,
  'Twas snatch'd by the Hero of Erie.

For the brave who have bled why indulge a vain sorrow?
  They were wreck'd on no *enemy's* coast ;
And some one of us may be welcom'd to-morrow,
  To Elysium by LAWRENCE'S ghost ;
Who, when call'd by Charon to take a short trip,
  With him in his crazy old wherry,
Saw his own dying orders "*Don't give up the Ship*"
  On the flag proudly floating o'er Perry.

Let each man round this board bid his children remember,
  With a gen'rous expansion of soul,
The glory that plays round the tenth of September,
  And crown its return with a bowl ;
Then the goblet shall foam, blow the wind high or low,
  And the heart be it mournful or merry,
And the purest of wine to the mem'ry shall flow
  Of the virtues and valor of Perry.

From Erie's Proudly Swelling Breast.

(Written by JOHN LATHROP, JR., Esq.)

[Tune : " Rise, Columbia."]

From Erie's proudly swelling breast,
  Exulting shouts of victory rise ;
The naval glories of the West,
  Outshine the beams of orient skies —
    Columbia's youthful heroes claim
    Eternal gratitude and fame !

Her dauntless Nelson, Nile no more,
  Unequall'd in his feats, shall boast—
Nor Trafalgar's immortal shore,
  Nor bold St. Vincent's laurell'd coast—
    One mighty deed has seal'd the claim
    Of Erie, to superior fame !

Perry—'twas thine, illustrious chief,
  To soothe thy dear Columbia's heart,
And o'er her gloomy cloud of grief,
  A brilliant ray of joy to dart—
    To raise the splendor of her name
    Beyond the pride of ancient fame!

Nor shall thy act of high emprise,
  Alone employ the festal song;
The pearly gems of pity's eyes,
  With valor's wreath to thee belong—
    Their blended beauties prove thy claim,
    To generous Scipio's spotless fame.

Th' historic Muse to future time,
  Shall bear thy triumphs in her lays,
And bards of every age and clime,
  With raptur'd breasts, shall chant thy praise.
    Thine, is thy country's love—thy name—
    Appals her foes—preserves her fame!

The Battle of Mobile Bay.

On the fifth of August, about two in the morning,
  All hands were aroused to prepare for the fray;
All being ready, as the day was just dawning,
  We opened the fight without any delay.

Our ships were in couples, to secure their protection,
  When the *Hartford* made signal to get under way;
Our guns were cast loose and decks cleared for action,
  As the fleet hove up anchor to enter the bay.

At each mast-head our banner was gallantly streaming—
  That gallant old banner, the Stripes and the Stars;
And may it thus ever aloft be found beaming,
  Defended by our gallant American tars!

We steered for Fort Morgan and, proudly advancing,
  The sloop-of-war *Brooklyn* was leading the van,
While the rebels supposed they surely could sink her
  With their forts and torpedoes, their gunboats and rams.

The fort opened fire determined to affright us,
  The *Brooklyn* replying, the action begun ;
The rebels soon found 'twas no use to fight us :
  Of vessels which entered we lost only one.

Brave Craven is gone, but his name we will cherish ;
  He went down with his ship ere the victory was won.
We mourn, too, the loss of his brave crew who perished
  In a watery grave, each man at his gun.

The fight was soon over, our fleet was victorious,
  We had captured Fort Morgan, Fort Gaines, and the ram ;
And Buchannan, of *Merrimac* fame so notorious,
  Was a prisoner in hands of our good Uncle Sam.

To shipmates who fell we give love's true devotion,
  We deplore their sad fate, hold their memory dear ;
Their loss daily mourn, felled in battle's commotion,
  And crown with affection's test, a sailor's sad tear.

Deathless the fame of brave Farragut, Commander !
  All ages will brighten laurels he dearly won,
The crowned heads of Europe looked on in deep wonder,
  While Columbia feels proud to have had such a son.

Since peace has brought blessing, our services over,
  Now at home with our families, our sweethearts and friends;
Should the cloud of grim war o'er our heads again hover,
  We'll be ready and cheerful the flag to defend.

The U. S. S. Kearsarge (Captain Winslow), and the Confederate Cruiser Alabama (Capt. Semmes).

(Action fought off Cherbourg, France, June 19th, 1864.)

It was early Sunday morning, in the year of sixty-four,
 The *Alabama* she steam'd out along the Frenchman's shore.
  Long time she cruised about,
  Long time she held her sway,
But now beneath the Frenchman's shore she lies off Cherbourg Bay.
  Hoist up the flag, and long may it wave
  Over the Union, the home of the brave!
  Hoist up the flag, and long may it wave,
  God bless America, the home of the brave!

The Yankee cruiser hove in view, the *Kearsarge* was her name,
 It ought to be engraved, in full, upon the scroll of fame;
  Her timbers made of Yankee oak,
  And her crew of Yankee tars,
And o'er her mizzen peak she floats the glorious stripes and stars.
  Hoist up the flag, and long may it wave
  Over the Union, the home of the brave!
  Hoist up the flag, and long may it wave,
  God bless America, the home of the brave!

A challenge unto Captain Semmes, bold Winslow he did send!
 "Bring on your *Alabama*, and to her we will attend,
  For we think your boasting privateer
  Is not so hard to whip;
And we'll show you that the *Kearsarge* is not a merchant ship."
  Hoist up the flag, and long may it wave
  Over the Union, the home of the brave!
  Hoist up the flag, and long may it wave,
  God bless America, the home of the brave!

It was early Sunday morning, in the year of sixty-four,
 The *Alabama* she stood out and cannons loud did roar;
The *Kearsarge* stood undaunted, and quickly she replied
 And let a Yankee 'leven-inch shell go tearing through her side.
  Hoist up the flag, and long may it wave
  Over the Union, the home of the brave!
  Hoist up the flag, and long may it wave,
  God bless America, the home of the brave!

The *Kearsarge* then she wore around and broadside on did bear,
  With shot and shell and right good-will, her timbers she did tear;
When they found that they were sinking, down came the stars and bars,
For the rebel gunners could not stand the glorious stripes and stars.
        Hoist up the flag, and long may it wave,
        Over the Union, the home of the brave!
        Hoist up the flag, and long may it wave,
        God bless America, the home of the brave!

The *Alabama* she is gone, she'll cruise the seas no more,
She met the fate she well deserved along the Frenchman's shore;
Then here is luck to the *Kearsarge*, we know what she can do,
Likewise to Captain Winslow and his brave and gallant crew.
        Hoist up the flag, and long may it wave
        Over the Union, the home of the brave!
        Hoist up the flag, and long may it wave,
        God bless America, the home of the brave!

The Varuna (Captain Boggs).

Sunk at the battle of New Orleans, April 24th, 1862.

(GEORGE H. BOKER.)

Who has not heard of the dauntless *Varuna?*
  Who has not heard of the deeds she has done?
Who shall not hear, while the brown Mississippi
  Rushes along from the snow to the sun?

Crippled and leaking she entered the battle,
  Sinking and burning she fought through the fray;
Crushed were her sides and the waves ran across her,
  Ere like a death-wounded lion at bay,
Sternly she closed in the last fatal grapple,
  Then in her triumph moved grandly away.

Five of the rebels, like satellites round her,
    Burned in her orbit of splendor and fear;
One, like the Pleiad of mystical story,
    Shot, terror-stricken, beyond her dread sphere.

We who are waiting with crowns for the victors,
    Though we should offer the wealth of our store,
Load the *Varuna* from deck down to kelson,
    Still would be niggard such tribute to pour
On courage so boundless. It beggars possession,—
    It knocks for just payment at Heaven's bright door!

Cherish the heroes who fought the *Varuna;*
    Treat them as kings if they honor your way;
Succor and comfort the sick and the wounded;
    Oh! for the dead let us all kneel and pray!

We Are Coming, Father Abra'am.

We are coming, Father Abra'am, three hundred thousand more,
From Mississippi's winding stream and from New England's shore;
We leave our ploughs and workshops, our wives and children dear,
With hearts too full for utterance, with but a silent tear:
We dare not look behind us, but steadfastly before.

    We are coming, Father Abra'am, three hundred thousand more!
    We are coming, we are coming, our Union to restore;
    We are coming, Father Abra'am, three hundred thousand more!

If you look across the hill-tops that meet the Northern sky,
Long moving lines of rising dust your vision may descry;
And now the wind, an instant, tears the cloudy veil aside,
And floats aloft our spangled flag, in glory and in pride;
And bayonets in the sunlight gleam, and bands brave music pour,
We are coming, Father Abra'am, three hundred thousand more!
              We are coming, &c.

If you look up our valleys, where the growing harvests shine,
You may see our sturdy farmer boys fast forming into line;
And children at their mothers' knees are pulling at the weeds,
And learning how to reap and sow against their country's needs;
And a farewell group stands weeping at every cottage door,
We are coming, Father Abra'am, three hundred thousand more!
              We are coming, &c.

You have called us, and we're coming, by Richmond's bloody tide,
To lay us down for freedom's sake, our brothers' bones beside ;
Or from foul treason's savage group to wrench the murderous blade,
And in the face of foreign foes its fragments to parade.
Six hundred thousand loyal men and true have gone before ;
We are coming, Father Abra'am, three hundred thousand more !

    We are coming, &c.

Perry's Victory.

September 10th, 1813.

O'er the bosom of Erie, in fanciful pride,
Did the fleet of Old England exultingly ride,
Till the flag of Columbia her Perry unfurl'd,
The boast of the West, and the pride of the world.

    CHORUS.

 And still should the foe dare the fight to sustain,
 Gallant Perry shall lead on to conquest again.

The spirit of Lawrence his influence speeds
To the van of the fight while the *Lawrence* he leads ;
There Death dealt around, though such numbers oppose,
And leveled the gun at fair Liberty's foes.

    And still, &c.

When covered with slain, from her decks he withdrew,
And led the *Niagara* the fight to renew ;
Where undaunted in danger our sea-beaten tars
O'er the cross of St. George waved the stripes and the stars !

Six ships, while our banners triumphantly flew,
Submitted to tars who were born to subdue ;
When they rushed to the battle, resolved to maintain
The freedom if trade and our right to the main !

With the glory of conquest our heroes are crowned,
Let their brows with the bright naval chaplet be bound!
For still should the foe dare the fight to sustain,
Gallant Perry shall lead them to conquest again.

Tacking Ship off Fire Island Light.

(WALTER MITCHELL.)

The weather leech of the topsail shivers,
   The bowlines strain and the lee shrouds slacken,
The braces are taut, the lithe boom quivers,
   And the waves with the coming squall-cloud blacken.

Open one point on the weather bow,
   Is the lighthouse tall on Fire Island Head;
There's a shade of doubt on the captain's brow,
   And the pilot watches the heaving lead.

The ship bends lower before the breeze,
   As her broadside fair to the blast she lays;
And she swifter springs on the rising seas,
   As the pilot calls, "Stand by for stays!"

Then, "Silence all!" as each in his place,
   With the gathered coil in his hardened hands,
By tack and bowline, by sheet and brace,
   Waiting the watchword, impatient stands.

And the light on Fire Island Head draws near,
   As, trumpet-winged, the pilot's shout
From his post on the bowsprit heel, I hear,
   With the welcome call of "Ready, about!"

No time to spare—it is touch and go,
    And the captain growls, " Down helm ! Hard down ! "
As my weight on the whirling spokes I throw,
    While the heavens grow black with the storm-cloud's frown.

High o'er the knight-heads flies the spray,
    As she meets the shock of the plunging sea ;
And my shoulder stiff to the wheel I lay,
    As I answer, " Aye, Aye, sir ! Hard a-lee ! "

With the swerving leap of a startled steed,
    The ship flies fast in the eye of the wind ;
The dangerous shoals on the lee recede,
    And the headlands white we leave behind.

The topsails flutter, the jibs collapse,
    And belly and tug at the groaning cleats ;
The spanker slats, and the mainsail flaps,
    And thunders the order, " Tacks and sheets ! "

'Mid the rattle of blocks and the tramp of the crew,
    Hisses the rain of the rushing squall ;
The sails are aback from clew to clew,
    And now is the moment for " Mainsail haul ! "

And the heavy yards, like a baby's toy,
    By fifty strong arms are swiftly swung ;
She holds her way, and I look with joy,
    For the first white spray o'er the bulwarks flung

" Let go and haul ! "—'tis the last command,
    And the head sails fill to the blast once more ;
Astern and to leeward lies the land,
    With its breakers white on the shingly shore.

What matters the reef, or the rain, or the squall,
    I steady the helm for the open sea—
The first mate clamors, " Belay there all ! "
    And the captain's breath once more comes free.

And so off shore let the good ship fly—
   Little care I how the gusts may blow,
In my forecastle bunk in a jacket dry—
   Eight bells have struck and my watch is below.

Farragut.

(By Shipmate Comrade J. W. BRYCE.)

His was the daring of the old Viking,
   A courage constant, confident, sublime,
   Which knew no obstacle of tide or time.
He deemed it but a light and common thing,
When the wild waves aloft their crests would fling,
And through the darkness came the fearful roar
   Of hungry breakers on the dread lee shore—
   While sailors heard the death-bell's warning chime,
Calm and unmoved his watchful post to keep,
And guide his bark in safety o'er the deep.

When furious raged the battle's thunder-storm,
   And the fierce, hurtling death-bolts shrieked aloud—
   The gallant fleet wrapp'd in a sulph'rous shroud—
High borne aloft was seen his manly form,
While played around his head the lightnings warm,
As bravely he surveyed the scene afar,
To mark the daring foeman's plan of war—
   Piercing with eagle eye the lurid cloud.
Then rang his voice, as clarion, loud and free,
To guide the fight, and herald victory!

Gentle as brave of heart —" tender and true "—
   Not Douglas had a more chivalric soul—
   More clear and prompt 'neath duty's high control.
No thought of low ambition's wiles he knew;
Cast in the old heroic mould, how few
Who tread the ever toilsome paths of fame,
Have left to future times so bright a name,
   Or won so high a place on honor's roll!
For men, while noble deeds have blazonry,
May ne'er forget the BAYARD OF THE SEA!

Ben Block.

Ben Block was a sailor as brave as could be,
  And Nan, faithful Nanny, was his wife,
And seven boys for the ocean had he,
  And he loved them as dear as his life;
Then Ben, as he thought, had enough for them all,
  Till fortune, that slippery jade,
One night shipwreck'd all he was worth in a squall,
  And poor Ben a beggar was made!

Yet think not he whimpered, or shrunk from man,
  No, Ben was as brave as before;
His life was preserved for his true-hearted Nan,
  And he scorned what was lost to deplore;
Besides, cried the tar, not a boy have I now,
  But can die for his country and king;
I can work, so can Nan, and show fortune as how,
  In spite of her frowns we can sing.

'Twas thus, argued Ben, as he sat on a rock,
  Near which his trim vessel went down,
And the hand which had snatched from the billows
    Ben Block,
  Determined his wishes to crown;
For Ben at that moment, his eyes stretching far,
  Beheld a white sail heave in view,
Which reached him, and took in a poor shipwreck'd tar,
  To join with a jolly ship's crew.

I thought so, said Ben, as he sprung on deck,
  A sailor should never despair;
Besides, as you see, I am saved from the wreck,
  And so I am still fortune's care!
You are, said a tar, as he grappled his hand,
  'Twas a messmate he'd once saved from jail,
For now I can pay what I owe, when I land,
  So cheerily, my heart, let us sail.

Ben dropp'd on his knee, sent a prayer up aloft,
  Called Providence watchful and kind,
Then cried to the friend he had sailed with so oft,
  We tars are oft shook with the wind;

But what matters that, there's an angel unseen,
  Will take us poor sailors in tow,
And, when we're in danger, will e'er step between
  Till death lets the sheet anchor go.

The Larboard Watch.

(WILLIAMS.)

At dreary midnight's cheerless hour,
  Deserted e'en by Cynthia's beam,
When tempests beat, and torrents pour,
  And twinkling stars no longer gleam;
The wearied sailor spent with toil
  Clings firmly to the weather shroud,
And still the lengthened hour to guile,
And still the lengthened hour to guile,
  Sings as he views the gath'ring clouds,
  Sings as he views the gath'ring clouds.
    Larboard Watch, ahoy!
    Larboard Watch, ahoy!
But who can speak the joy he feels,
While o'er the foam his vessel reels,
And his tired eyelids slumb'ring fall,
He rouses at the welcome call
Of Larboard Watch, ahoy!
Larboard Watch, Larboard Watch,
    Larboard Watch, ahoy!

With anxious care he eyes each wave
  That swelling threatens to o'erwhelm,
And his storm-beaten bark to save,
  Directs with skill the faithful helm.
With joy he drinks the cheering grog
  'Mid storms that bellow loud and hoarse,
With joy he heaves the reeling log,
With joy he heaves the reeling log,
  And marks the leeway and the course,
  And marks the leeway and the course.
    Larboard Watch, ahoy! &c.

The Sailor.

(WALTER COTTON. Born, 1801. Sometime Chaplain U. S. Navy.)

A sailor ever loves to be in motion,
    Roaming about he scarce knows where or why ;
He looks upon the dim and shadowy ocean
    As home, abhors the land ; and e'en the sky,
Boundless and beautiful, has naught to please
Except some clouds, which promise him a breeze.

He is a child of mere impulse and passion,
    Loving his friends and generous to his foes,
And fickle as the most ephemeral fashion
    Save in the cut and color of his clothes,
And in a set of phrases, which on land
The wisest head could never understand.

He thinks his dialect the very best
    That ever flowed from any human lip,
And whether in his prayers, or at a jest,
    Uses the terms for managing a ship ;
And even in death would order up the helm,
In hope to clear the " undiscovered realm."

He makes a friend where'er he meets a shore,
    One whom he cherishes with some affection ;
But leaving port, he thinks of her no more,
    Unless it be, perchance, in some reflection
Upon his wicked ways, then with a sigh,
Resolves on reformation—ere he die.

In calms, he gazes at the sleeping sea,
    Or seeks his lines, and sets himself to angling,
Or takes to politics, and, being free
    Of facts and full of feeling, falls to wrangling ;
Then recollects a distant eye and lip,
And rues the day on which he saw a ship.

Then looks up to the sky to watch each cloud,
    As it displays its faint and fleeting form ;
Then o'er the calm begins to mutter loud,
    And swears he would exchange it for a storm,
Tornado, anything—to put a close
To this most dead, monotonous repose.

An order given, and he obeys, of course,
    Though it were to run his ship upon the rocks—
Capture a squadron with a boat's-crew force—
    Or batter down the massive granite blocks
Of some huge fortress with a swivel, pike,
    Pistol, aught that will throw a ball, or strike.

He never shrinks, whatever may betide ;
    His weapon may be shiver'd in his hand,
His last companion shot down by his side,
    Still he maintains his firm and desperate stand—
Bleeding and battling—with his colors fast
As nail can bind them to his shatter'd mast.

Such men fall not unmourn'd—their winding sheet
    May be the ocean's deep, unresting wave ;
Yet o'er their grave will wandering minds repeat
    The dirge of millions for the fallen brave ;
While each high deed survives in holier trust,
Than those consigned to mound or marble bust.

I love the sailor—his eventful life—
    His generous spirit—his contempt of danger—
His firmness in the gale, the wreck, and strife ;
    And though a wild and reckless ocean ranger,
God grant he make that port, when life is o'er,
Where storms are hush'd, and billows break no more.

Our Yankee. Ships.

[Air: "A Wet Sheet," &c.]

Our Yankee ships in fleet career,
   They linger not behind,
Where gallant sails from other lands
   Court favoring tide and wind.
With banners on the breeze they leap
   As gaily o'er the foam,
As stately barks from prouder seas,
   That long have learned to roam.

   Our Yankee ships, &c.

The Indian wave with luring smiles,
   Sweep round them bright to-day,
And havens to Atlantic Isles
   Are opening on their way.
Ere yet these evening shadows close,
   Or this frail song is o'er,
Full many a straining mast will rise
   To greet a foreign shore.

   Our Yankee ships, &c.

High up the lashing northern deep,
   Where glimmering watch-lights beam,
Away in beauty where the stars
   In tropic brightness gleam;
Where'er the sea-bird wets her beak,
   Or blows the stormy gale,
On to the water's farthest verge
   Our ships majestic sail.

   Our Yankee ships, &c.

They dip their keels in every stream
 That swells beneath the sky ;
And where old ocean billows roll,
 Their lofty pennants fly.
They furl their sheets in threat'ning clouds,
 That float across the main,
To link with love earth's distant bays,
 In many a golden chain.

  Our Yankee ships, &c.

The Seaman's Lay.

[Tune : "Oh, No, We Never Mention Her."]

List, shipmates, to a seaman's lay ;
 Jack Temperance and Jack Grog
Are gallant sailors in their way,
 As ever hove a log ;
But Grog's a lad of fits and starts ;
 You'll find him sharp and slow ;
Now hot, now cold : his spirits up,
 He's all for dash and blow.

But if at times he's sharp and quick,
 'Tis soon he'll flag and tire ;
And then so hot, he'd eat Old Nick,
 Or set the sea on fire.
And though you hear him brag full oft,
 He bangs the other hollow,
I never knew him go aloft,
 When Temperance would not follow.

But when he's had the drop he likes—
 He loves his glass we know—
The squall comes on—the boatswain pipes
 All hands to reef and stow ;
'Tis then aloft and lying out,
 To reef, or stow, or bend,
Jack Temperance has the ready hand,
 To stay his falling friend.

Oh, Temperance is a seaman bold
   As ever trod the deck ;
And oft when seas like mountains roll'd,
   Has saved the ship from wreck ;
And when there rolls that mountain sea,
   All threat'ning to o'erwhelm,
While breakers thunder on the lee,
   Let Temperance take the helm.

The Yankee Man-of-War.

(W. J. HENDERSON.)

We ride head to wind and the breeze whistles free,
The land is to windward, the sea's on our lee.
Man the bars and heave taut, off stoppers, heave round !
Clear the jib, port your helm ; now the anchor breaks ground.

Lay aloft, you sail loosers ! Man halliard and sheet !
There's nothing can catch our fair lady so fleet.
We're bound for the uttermost rim of the day ;
Lay down from aloft ! Now sheet home, hoist away !

We are running off soundings, the wind hauls a-beam ;
Along the horizon there comes a white gleam.
We'll take off the stu'nsails and still onward spin :
So lower away now ! Haul down and rig in !

The wind comes ahead and the jib falls a-back ;
Now ready about ! 'Tis the order to tack.
Hard a-lee ! From the quarter-deck echoes the call :
It's raise tacks and sheets ! Haul taut ! Mainsail haul !

Up yonder to windward the clouds darkly frown ;
Man clewlines and buntlines ! Look lively ! Clew down !
The gale is upon us with riot and rout !
'Loft topmen ! Come, cheer'ly ! Trice up and lay out !

At last to the southward the swift gale has whirled,
Once more to fair breezes our sails are unfurled ;
At the masthead the lookout swings wide to and fro,
Till the silence is rent with the warning, "Sail ho !"

Then hark ! The sharp beat of the hollow-voiced drum ;
To quarters ! See yonder, the enemy's come.
Our colors break out. Oh, the foe woe betide !
To quarters ! Now silence ! Cast loose and provide !

Run in, serve and sponge ! Load, run out, and prime !
Now point, ready, fire ! There are smoke, blood, and grime.
But down come her colors ; she yields to our pluck ;
Raise cheer upon cheer ! She is ours ! She has struck !

Farewell to Grog.

(CASPAR SCHENCK, U. S. Navy.)

Scene Ward-room of U. S. S.——— Time, night of August 31st, 1862. The law abolishing grog taking effect September 1st, 1862.

[Air : "Come, Landlord, Fill the Flowing Bowl."]

  Come, messmates, pass the bottle 'round ;
   Our time is short, remember,
  For our grog must stop and our spirits drop
   On the first day of September.

  Farewell, Old Rye, 'tis a sad, sad word,
   But, alas ! it must be spoken,
  The ruby cup must be given up,
   And the Demijohn be broken.

  Jack's happy days will soon be gone,
   To return again, oh ! never,
  For they've raised his pay five cents a day,
   But stopped his grog forever.

Yet memory oft will backward turn,
  And dwell, with fondness partial,
On the days when gin was not a sin,
  Nor cocktails brought Court Martial.

(Boatswain's Mate pipes " All hands splice the main braces.")

All hands to splice the main brace call,
  But splice it now in sorrow,
For the spirit-room key will be laid away
  Forever on to-morrow.

Though Lost to Sight, to Memory Dear.

(GEORGE LINLEY, Greenwich Magazine for Marines, 1701.)

Sweetheart, good-bye! the fluttering sail
  Is spread, to waft me far from thee;
And soon, before the favoring gale,
  My ship shall bound upon the sea.
Perchance, all desolate and forlorn,
  These eyes shall miss thee many a year;
But unforgotten every charm:
  Though lost to sight, to memory dear.

Sweetheart, good-bye! one last embrace:
  O, cruel fate! true souls to sever;
Yet in this heart's most sacred place
  Thou, thou alone, shall dwell forever.
And still shall recollection trace,
  In fancy's mirror, ever near,
Each smile, each tear, that form, that face:
  Though lost to sight, to memory dear.

The Wasp's Frolic.

October 20th, 1812.

(From " Naval Songster," 1815.)

'Twas on board the sloop-of-war *Wasp*, boys,
   We set sail from Delaware Bay,
To cruise on Columbia's fair coast, sirs,
   Our rights to maintain on the sea.

Three days were not past on our station,
   When the *Frolic* came up to our view;
Says Jones, " Show the flag of our nation ; "
   Three cheers were then given by our crew.

We boldly bore up to this Briton,
   Whose cannon began for to roar ;
The *Wasp* soon her stings from her side ran,
   When we on them a broadside did pour.

Each sailor stood firm at his quarters,
   'Twas minutes past forty and three,
When fifty bold Britons were slaughter'd,
   Whilst our guns swept their masts in the sea.

Their breasts then with valor still glowing,
   Acknowledged the battle we'd won,
On us then bright laurels bestowing,
   When to leeward they fired a gun.

On their decks we the twenty guns counted,
   With a crew for to answer the same ;
Eighteen was the number we mounted,
   Being served by the lads of true game.

With the *Frolic* in tow we were standing,
   All in for Columbia's fair shore ;
But fate on our laurels was frowning,
   Were taken by a seventy-four.

The Enterprise and Boxer.

September 4th, 1813.

(From " Naval Songster," 1815.)

Ho! all ye brave tars of Columbia,
   That for your country do fight,
The rays of fam'd glory shines on you,
   That are most brilliantly bright.

The *Enterprise* brig of our Navy,
   With a crew undaunted and brave,
Fell in with the British brig *Boxer*,
   And she box'd her men to their grave.

Loud roar'd the *Enterprise* cannon,
   And death to the *Boxer* was hurl'd;
Her guns spoke the rights of our seamen,
   And echoed Free Trade to the world!

Their valor for boxing then ceased,
   Acknowledg'd the battle we'd won;
Their ship being so much disabled,
   She quickly stopt firing a gun.

Johnny Bull send no more of your *Boxers*
   Unto Columbia's fair shore,
Lest they get their daylights knock'd out,
   And can't see their homes any more.

Our Rights we will never surrender,
   While a ship can float on the main;
Free Trade is the Right we contend for,
   This right we still will maintain.

Our Navy.

1813.

[Tune: "Hail, Liberty."]

On wings of glory, swift as light,
    The sound of battle came,
The gallant Hull in glorious fight,
    Has won the wreath of fame.
Let brave Columbia's noble band,
    With hearts united rise,
Swear to protect their native land,
    Till sacred Freedom dies.

Let brave Decatur's dauntless breast
    With patriot ardor glow,
And in the garb of victory drest,
    Triumphant, blast the foe.
    Let brave, &c.

And Rodgers, with his gallant crew,
    O'er the wide ocean ride,
To prove their loyal spirit true,
    And crush old Albion's pride.
    Let brave, &c.

Then hail another *Guerriere* there,
    With roaring broadsides hail,
And while the thunder rends the air,
    See Britain's sons turn pale.
    Let brave, &c.

The day is ours, my boys, huzza!
    The great Commander cries,
While all responsive roar huzza!
    With pleasure-sparkling eyes.
    Let brave, &c.

Thus shall Columbia's fame be spread,
Her Heaven-born eagle soar,
Her deeds of glory shall be read
When tyrants are no more.

Let brave, &c.

The United States and the Macedonian.

The *United States*, 44 (Captain Stephen Decatur), while cruising near the Island of Madeira, fell in with and captured the British 38-gun frigate *Macedonian* (Captain J. S. Carden), October 25th, 1812.

The banner of Freedom high floated unfurled,
While the silver-tipt surges in low homage curled,
Flashing bright round the bow of Decatur's brave bark,
In contest, an "eagle"—in chasing, a "lark."
    The bold *United States*,
      Which four-and-forty rates,
Will ne'er be known to yield—be known to yield or fly,
Her motto is, "Glory! we conquer or we die."

All canvas expanded to woo the coy gale,
The ship cleared for action, in chase of a sail;
The foeman in view, every bosom beats high,
All eager for conquest, or ready to die.
    The bold *United States*,
      Which four-and-forty rates,
Will ne'er be known to yield—be known to yield or fly,
Her motto is, "Glory! we conquer or we die."

Now havoc stands ready, with optics of flame,
And battle-hounds "strain on the start" for the game;
The blood-demons rise on the surge for their prey,
While Pity, rejected, awaits the dread fray.
    The bold *United States*,
      Which four-and-forty rates,
Will ne'er be known to yield—be known to yield or fly,
Her motto is "Glory! we conquer or we die."

The gay floating streamers of Britain appear,
Waving light on the breeze as the stranger we near;
And now could the quick-sighted Yankee discern
"*Macedonian*," emblazoned at large on her stern.
    The bold *United States*,
      Which four-and-forty rates,
Will ne'er be known to yield—be known to yield or fly,
Her motto is "Glory! we conquer or we die."

She wait'd our approach, and the contest began,
But to waste ammunition is no Yankee plan;
In awful suspense every match was withheld,
While the bull-dogs of Britain incessantly yelled.
    The bold *United States*,
      Which four-and-forty rates,
Will ne'er be known to yield—be known to yield or fly,
Her motto is "Glory! we conquer or we die."

Unawed by her thunders, alongside we came,
While the foe seemed enwrapped in a mantle of flame;
When prompt to the word, such a flood we return,
That Neptune, aghast, thought his trident would burn.
    The bold *United States*,
      Which four-and-forty rates,
Will ne'er be known to yield—be known to yield or fly,
Her motto is "Glory! we conquer or we die."

Now the lightning of battle gleams horridly red,
With a tempest of iron and hail-storm of lead;
And our fire on the foe we so copiously poured,
His mizzen and topmasts soon went by the board.
    The bold *United States*,
      Which four-and-forty rates,
Will ne'er be known to yield—be known to yield or fly,
Her motto is "Glory! we conquer or we die."

So fierce and so bright did our flashes aspire,
The thought that their cannon had set us on fire,
"The Yankee's in flames!"—every British tar hears,
And hails the false omen with three hearty cheers.
    The bold *United States*,
        Which four-and-forty rates,
Will ne'er be known to yield—be known to yield or fly,
Her motto is "Glory! we conquer or we die."

In seventeen minutes they found their mistake,
And were glad to surrender and fall in our wake;
Her decks were with carnage and blood deluged o'er,
Where, welt'ring in blood, lay an hundred and four.
    The bold *United States*,
        Which four-and-forty rates,
Will ne'er be known to yield—be known to yield or fly,
Her motto is "Glory! we conquer or we die."

But though she was made so completely a wreck,
With blood they had scarcely encrimsoned our deck;
Only five valiant Yankees in the contest were slain,
And our ship in five minutes refitted again.
    The bold *United States*,
        Which four-and-forty rates,
Will ne'er be known to yield—be known to yield or fly,
Her motto is "Glory! we conquer or we die."

Let Britain no longer lay claim to the seas,
For the trident of Neptune is ours, if we please,
While Hull and Decatur and Jones are our boast,
We dare their whole navy to come on our coast.
    The bold *United States*,
        Which four-and-forty rates,
Will ne'er be known to yield—be known to yield or fly,
Her motto is "Glory! we conquer or we die."

Rise, tars of Columbia!—and share in the fame,
Which gilds Hull's, Decatur's, and Jones' bright name;
Fill a bumper, and drink, "Here's success to the cause,
But Decatur supremely deserves our applause."
    The bold *United States*,
    Which four-and-forty rates,
Shall ne'er be known to yield—be known to yield or fly,
Her motto is "Glory! we conquer or we die."

The Land of Liberty.

(ANONYMOUS.)

I love my country's vine-clad hills,
Her thousand bright and gushing rills,
    Her sunshine and her storms,
Her rough and rugged rocks that rear
Their hoary heads high in the air,
    In wild, fantastic forms.

I love her rivers deep and wide,
Those mighty streams that seaward glide
    To seek the ocean's breast,
Her smiling fields, her flowery dales,
Her shady dells, her pleasant vales,
    Abodes of peaceful rest.

I love her forests dark and lone,
For there the wild-bird's merry tone
    I hear from morn to night;
And lovelier flowers are there, I ween,
Than e'er in Eastern lands were seen,
    In varied colors bright.

Her forests and her valleys fair,
Her flowers that scent the morning air,
    All have their charms for me;
But more I love my country's name,
Those words that echo deathless fame,—
    The land of Liberty!

The Brandywine.

(Mediterranean, 1840.)

Come wreathe the goblet with the vine,
Ye gallant sons of the *Brandywine;*
   To all our hearts,
   That name imparts,
An impulse half divine.

CHORUS.

Brandywine, Brandywine,
Oh! the roaring Brandy, *Brandywine.*

Our course is o'er the trackless deep,
The billows cradle us to sleep,
   But joy is there,
   Our hearts to cheer,
Aboard the *Brandywine.*—CHO.

Our sweethearts, wives, and children dear,
Tho' distant far, to memory near,
But joy is there, our hearts to cheer,
   Aboard the *Brandywine.*—CHO.

When we return from distant seas,
We'll take our children on our knees,
And kiss the lass, and drink a glass
   To the roaring *Brandywine.* – CHO.

Kingdom Coming.

(Key of E Flat.)

Say, darkies, hab you seen old massa,
   Wid de muffstash on his face,
Go long de road some time dis mornin',
   Like he gwine to leab de place?

He seen a smoke, way up de ribber,
    Whar de Linkum gunboats lay;
He took his hat, an' lef berry sudden,
    An' I spec he's run away!

Chorus.

De massa run! ha, ha!
    De darkey stay! ho, ho!
It mus' be now de kingdom comin',
    An' de year ob Jubilo!
It mus' be now de kingdom comin',
    An' de year ob Jubilo!

He six foot one way, four foot tudder,
    An' he weigh tree hundred pound,
His coat so big, he couldn't pay de tailor,
    An' it won't go half-way round.
He drill so much dey call him Cap'n,
    An' he get so drefful tann'd,
I spec he try an' fool dem Yankees
    For to tink he's contraband.—Cho.

De darkies feel so lonesone libbing
    In de log house on de lawn,
Dey move dar tings to massa's parlor
    For to keep it while he's gone;
Dar's wine an' cider in de kitchen,
    An' de darkies dey'll hab some;
I spose dey'll all be cornfiscated,
    When de Linkum gun-boats come.—Cho.

De oberseer he make us trouble,
    An' he dribe us round a spell;
We lock him up in de smoke-house cellar,
    Wid de key trown down de well.
De whip is lost, de han'cuff broken,
    But the massa 'll hab his pay;
He's old enough, big enough, ought to know better,
    Dan to went an' run away.—Cho.

The Flag.

(JAMES WHITCOMB RILEY.)

The ocean guarded flag of light, forever may it fly ;
It flashed o'er Monmouth's bloody fight, and lit McHenry's sky ;
It bears upon its folds of flame to earth's remotest wave
The names of men whose deeds of fame shall e're inspire the brave.

Timbers have crashed and guns have pealed beneath its radiant glow,
But never did that ensign yield its honor to the foe ;
Its fame shall march with martial tread down ages yet to be,
To guard these stars that never paled in fight on land or sea.

Its stripes of red, eternal dyed with heart-streams of all lands ;
Its white, the snow-capped hills that hide in storm their upraised hands ;
Its blue, the ocean waves that beat 'round freedom's circled shore ;
Its stars, the steps of angels' feet that turn for evermore.

The Starry Flag Floats Free.

(STOCKTON BATES.)

[Tune: "Union."]

From proud Atlantic's surging waves,
    To where the broad Pacific lies,
And playfully the bright sand laves
    Beneath our clear and sunny skies ;
And far along Canadian lines,
    The rocky borders of the land,
To where the Gulf in beauty shines,
    And breaks in billows on the strand.

From Allegheny's crested mounts,
    And on the Rockies' summits gray,
Where, brightly, snow-fed crystal founts
    Are welling forth afresh alway.
On Mississippi's mighty tides,
    And on Ohio's silver stream,
Or where the Susquehanna glides,
    Or Schuylkill's laughing ripples gleam.

Where Delaware, with current grave,
    Is sweeping outward to the sea ;
In every land, on every wave,
    Aloft the Starry Flag floats free !
And through all time this flag above,
    In triumph o'er oppression's holds,
Shall, in the light of peace and love,
    Ever unroll its glorious folds.

The Flag Goes By.

(H. H. BENNETT.)

Hats off !
Along the street there comes
A blare of bugles, a ruffle of drums,
A flash of color beneath the sky.
Hats off !
The flag is passing by.

Blue and crimson and white it shines,
Over the steel-tipped, ordered lines ;
Hats off !
The colors before us fly ;
But more than the flag is passing by.

Sea fights and land fights grim and great,
Fought to make and to save the state;
Weary marches, and sinking ships;
Cheers of victory on dying lips.

Days of plenty and days of peace;
March of a strong land's swift increase;
Equal justice, right and law,
Stately honor and reverend awe.

Sign of a nation, great and strong,
To ward her people from foreign wrong;
Pride and glory and honor, all
Live in the colors to stand or fall.

Hats off!
Along the street there comes
A blare of bugles, a ruffle of drums;
And loyal hearts are beating high.
Hats off!
The flag is passing by.

The Banner of the Sea.

(D. BRAINERD WILLIAMS.)

Of all the flags that float aloft, o'er Neptune's gallant tars,
That wave on high in victory, above the sons of Mars,
Give us the flag, Columbia's flag, the emblem of the free,
Whose flashing stars blazed through our wars, for TRUTH and
    LIBERTY!

CHORUS.

Then dip it, lads, in ocean's brine, and give it three times three,
And fling it out, 'mid song and shout, the Banner of the Sea!
Then dip it, lads, in ocean's brine, and give it three times three,
And fling it out, 'mid song and shout, the Banner of the Sea!

Beneath its folds we fear no foe, our hearts shall never quail,
With bosoms bare, the storm we'll dare, and brave the battle gale;
And though the cannon plough our decks, the planks with gore run red,
Still through the fray, our flag alway, shall gleam far overhead.
CHO.

On every wave, to every shore, Columbia's flag shall go,
And through all time, its fame sublime, with brighter hues shall glow:
For Freedom's standard is our flag, its guardians, Freedom's sons,
And wo betide the insulter's pride, when we unloose our guns.
CHO.

Its enemies our own shall be, upon the land or main,
Its starry light shall gild the fight, and guide our iron rain.
Nor foreign power, nor treason's art, shall shake our patriot love,
While with our life. in peace or strife, we'll keep that flag above.
CHO.

The Jackets of Blue.

The lads are all singing,
The bells are all ringing,
The lasses are trimming their caps all anew;
The young and the old come,
The great and the small come,
And all for to welcome the jackets of blue.
They come from the war, far over the wave,
Oh! who would not fight 'neath the flag of the brave!
The poorest, the proudest the land can afford,
At the war-cry of Freedom will all draw the sword;
Then hurrah! hurrah! for the jackets of blue,
For the brave Yankee tars in their jackets of blue!

Each tar has a story
To tell of his glory,
In battles all glory, his duty to do;
Through climes still a ranger,
He braves every danger,
For fear is a stranger to jackets of blue.
His ship, trimmed so gaily, now gallantly rides,
With broad pennant waving—the Queen of the Tides!
The lasses all vow that none love so true,
As the brave Yankee tars, in their jackets of blue.

Our Navy.

(As written and sung by W. E. BURTON, at a dinner given to Commodore Conner, by the citizens of Philadelphia.)

Huzza for the wars, where the stripes and the stars
  From the mizzen peak cheerily waving,
The red, white, and blue, the pride of the true,
  The winds of the world dare be braving;
  When tyrants for conquest are craving,
  Our bunting for liberty waving,
With some Yankee thunder, will cause to knock under
  The foes who are freemen enslaving—
    For we have a nice little navy,
    A tight little, right little navy;
The world we can whip, for "Don't give up the ship,"
    Is the watchward of our little navy.

Its first institution, in *the* revolution,
  Said little for our little navy,
Till Dale and Paul Jones risked their blood and their bones,
  And roasted Old Bull in hot gravy;
Then Barney, and Biddle, and Barry,
Like busy *bees* played up old Harry;
And Truxton's bold station in the old *Constellation*,
Told Mounseer 'twas dangerous to tarry—
  For tho' then we'd not much of a navy,
  We knocked all our foes to Old Davy;
Ship, squadron, or fleet, it never was beat –
  And the Yankees are proud of their navy.

Then when the bold Turk gave our jolly tars work,
   And at Tripoli tribute demanded,
Then Stephen Decatur, that jolly first-rater,
   With Bainbridge and Preble was banded;
They kept up the pride of the navy,
They made the Turks sing out *peccavi*,
   They stopped off all ransom, and did the thing handsome—
     And the world wondered more at our navy—
     For then we'd a nice little navy,
     A tight little, right little navy;
The world we can whip, for "Don't give up the ship,"
   Is the watchword of our little navy.

My verse now will hit on the last war with Britain,
   Where Rodgers, and Lawrence, and Chauncey,
With Elliott and Perry, who fought at Lake Erie,
   And gave the foe all he could fancy.
Here's the triumphs of *Old Ironsides*, sirs,
The wonder and boast of the tide, sirs,
   For Stewart and Hull gave a glorious pull,
To make her the national pride, sirs.
     For she is well known in our navy,
     Our right little, tight little navy;
Ship, squadron, or fleet, it never was beat,
   And it never will be beat—will our navy!

It's not my intention each victory to mention,
   There'd never be an end to my story;
But Commodore Conner, whose name rhymes with honor,
   Must needs have his share of the glory.
In the *Hornet* he first raised his name up;
In the Gulf he has well kept his fame up,
When the troops he did land upon Mexico's strand,
   Then Scott could with ease make his game up.
     So drink a good time to the navy,
     For now we've a rousing good navy,
With officers brave, to rule o'er the wave,
   We never need fear for our navy.

The Topsails Shiver in the Wind.

The topsails shiver in the wind,
  Our ship she's cast to sea,
But yet my soul, my heart, my mind,
  Are, Mary, moor'd with thee ;
For though thy sailor's bound afar,
Still love shall be my leading star.

Should landsmen flatter, when we've sailed,
  Oh doubt their artful tales ;
No gallant sailor ever failed,
  If love breathed constant gales.
Thou art the compass of my soul,
Which steers my heart from pole to pole.

These are our cares ; but if you're kind,
  We'll scorn the dashing main,
The rocks, the billow, and the wind,
  Till we return again.
Now freedom's glory rests with you,
Our sails are full, sweet girl, adieu !

The Wave For Me.

The wave, the wave, the wave for me—
  A life upon the ocean,
When skies are dark, and our brave bark
  Hath all her wings in motion,
With naught except the tempest nigh,
And one bright star within the sky,
  To guide the seaman's roaming,
  When madden'd seas are foaming.

The wave, the wave, the crested wave,
　　When gloriously 'tis bounding—
The war-steed of the ocean-king,
　　With voice like thunder sounding.
'Tis then our snowy sails we furl,
And laugh to see the waters curl,
　　And tempests bleach the billow
　　That soon may be our pillow.

The bard may strike his sounding lyre,
　　And sing of landsmen's pleasures,
Of verdant fields, and mighty hills,
　　Of beauty, and of treasure;
But give to me the noble wave—
The seaman's home, the seaman's grave—
　　Within whose depths have slumber'd,
　　For ages, tars unnumber'd.

Sweet Goddess That Guides Us.

Sweet Goddess! that guides us to glory and fame,
　　And rides in the terrible blast,
Now give to our navy a glorious name,
　　That long as our country shall last.

The tars of Columbia were born to be brave,
　　Their birthright is liberty blest;
To shield it from insult, from ruin to save,
　　Shall long be the pride of each breast.

Huzza to the brave that triumphantly ride
　　And traverse the boisterous sea;
Columbia's glory, her honor and pride,
　　And Freedom's fair bulwark shall be.

Then hail to our navy, all honors bestow,
　　Our tars are both gallant and brave;
Success to our sailors, wherever they go,
　　And in death sweetest peace to their grave.

Did Dewey Do It?

(JOHN STANLEY.)

Victory of Manilla, won by Commodore George Dewey United States Navy, May 1st, 1898.

Well, now say, did Dewey do it?
   Well, I rather guess he did!
   For he lammed 'em, and he slammed 'em, and he
      rammed 'em plump amid ;
Till there wasn't left a Spaniard,
   Or a Spanish ship or crew,
   For he hailed 'em, and he nailed 'em, and he whaled
      'em black and blue.

Would that I had but been with him,
   When he met the Dons that day,
   At Manilla, o'er the biller, where their old flotilla lay ;
Wouldn't I have given 'em toco ;
   Wouldn't I have killed them Dons !
   I'd a-slashed 'em, I'd a-smashed 'em, I'd a-hashed the
      sons of guns !

Well, I wasn't there with Dewey,
   But he got there just the same ;
   Sent 'em scowling, sent 'em bowling, sent 'em howl-
      ing limp and lame ;
And I hope that at the roll call
   Satan gives them sons of Spain—
   They'll remember, and remember, and remember still,
      the *Maine !*

The Battle-Song of the Iowa.

While We are Fighting for Cuba.

(CLAY M. GREENE.)

[Air: "Marching Through Georgia."]

Clear the decks for action, boys; we're brave and strong and true!
Rouse again the loyal fire that burned in '62;
Strike a blow of vengeance for our murdered boys in blue,
    While we are fighting for Cuba.

REFRAIN.

Hurrah! Hurrah! Three times and once again!
Hurrah! Hurrah! The boasted power of Spain
Shall crumble 'neath our battle-cry, "Do not forget the *Maine*,"
    While we are fighting for Cuba.

Hail to stanch *Iowa*, boys, and hail to Fighting Bob;
All our guns are ready, and our engines beat and throb,
Waiting for an order to destroy that Spanish mob,
    While we are fighting for Cuba.

Take your lanyards in your hands, the Spaniard is in sight;
Like our gallant Captain, we are spoiling for a fight;
For our cause is mighty and we know that we are right,
    While we are fighting for Cuba.

Speed afar across the deep with loud and lusty yell;
Promise what our Captain did, as we have heard 'em tell;
Spanish in a month will be the "parley-voo" of hell,
    While we are fighting for Cuba.

Firm as rock our nerves, my lads, as you are taking aim;
They are only Spaniards, but the shots are worth the game;
Every one's a mark upon our country's roll of fame,
    While we are fighting for Cuba.

Thrill with every order, lads, and follow where you're led;
Don't forget the other days when Yankees fought and bled;
Sing the song of freedom and avenge our noble dead,
    While we are fighting for Cuba.

"Remember the Maine!"

(ROBERT BURNS WILSON.)

U. S. S. *Maine*, blown up in the Harbor of Havana, Cuba, while on a friendly visit to that port, February 15th, 1898, with a loss of two of her officers and 264 of her crew.

When vengeance awakes, when the battle breaks,
    And the ships sweep over the sea ;
When the foe is near'd, when the decks are cleared,
    And the colors floating free ;
When the Squadrons meet, when it's fleet to fleet,
    And front to front with Spain ;
From ship to ship, from lip to lip,
    Pass on the quick refrain,
        "Remember, remember the *Maine!*"

When the flag shall sign : "Advance in line,
    Trim ship on an even keel,"
When the guns shall flash, and the shot shall crash,
    And bound on the ringing steel ;
When the rattling blasts, from the armored masts,
    Are hurling their deadliest rain,
Let their voices loud, through the binding cloud,
    Cry, ever, the fierce refrain,
        "Remember, remember the *Maine!*"

God's sky and sea in that storm shall be
    Fate's chaos of smoke and flame,
But across that hell every shot shall tell,
    Not a gun can miss its aim ;
Not a blow will fail on the crumbling mail ;
    And the waves that engulf the slain
Shall sweep the decks of the blackened wrecks,
    With the thundering dread refrain,
        "Remember, remember the *Maine!*" *

* Copyright. Used by permission of Robert Howard Russell.

CONTENTS

A

	PAGE
A Bold, Brave Crew, on an Ocean Blue	111
About a Great Sea Snake You've Heard	132
Admiral, The Return of the	190
Alarmed Skipper, The	65
A Life on the Ocean Wave	159
All's Well	134
America (My Country, 'Tis of Thee)	8
America, Commerce, and Freedom	29
America, Long Live	93
American Boy	79
American Sailor	61
American Star, The	77
American Tar, The	95
An American Frigate, a Frigate of Fame (Paul Jones)	139
Angel's Whisper	129
Argo of Greece, that Brought the Fleece	85
As Near Beauteous Boston, Lying (Destruction of Tea, 1776)	104
As Slow our Ship her Foamy Track	158
A Song unto Liberty's Brave Buccaneer (Paul Jones)	110
As You Mean to Set Sail for the Land of Delight	126
At a Dinner to Admiral Farragut	19
A Union Ship and a Union Crew	76
Away, Away, I May Not Stand	145
A Wet Sheet and a Flowing Sea	123

B

Bainbridge's Tid-re I	100
Ballad of the Oysterman	67
Banner of the Sea, The	231
Banner of the Stars, The	56
Banner, Star-Spangled, The	6

	PAGE
Barney Buntline	148
Battle Chorus	78
Battle Hymn of the Republic	9
Battle of Mobile Bay	202
Battle of Lake Erie (We Sail'd To and Fro)	103
Battle of Lake Erie (O'er the Bosom of Erie)	207
Battle of Lake Champlain (Where Lordly Champlain)	109
Battle Song of the *Iowa*, The	238
Bay of Biscay, O!	136
Behold! How Brightly Breaks the Morning	118
Ben Block was a Sailor as Brave as Could be	211
Black-Eyed Susan	114
Blow High, Blow Low, Let Tempests Tear	165
Bonne Homme Richard and *Serapis*	105
Bound 'Prentice to a Waterman	117
Brandywine, The	227

C

Canadian Boat Song, The	138
Cease, Rude Boreas, Blustering Railer	151
Charlie Stewart, When a Youth, Left his Land and his Home,	87
Child of a Tar, The	163
Columbia Rules the Sea	24
Columbia, Arise to Glory	74
Come, Strike the bold Anthem, the War-Dogs are Howling	77
Comrades! Join the Flag of Glory	27
Come, Lads, draw Near	100
Come, Loose Every Sail to the Breeze	186
Constellation and the *Insurgente*	53
Constitution, The Frigate	85
Constitution and *Guerriere*	63, 119
Cumberland, The (H. W. Longfellow)	22
Cumberland, On Board the (Geo. W. Boker)	38

D

Deserted by the Waning Moon (All's Well)	134
Destruction of Tea—1776	104
Did Dewey Do It?	237
Disturb Not his Slumbers, let Washington Sleep	83

E

	PAGE
E Pluribus Unum	88
Enterprise and *Boxer*, The	221

F

Faintly as Tolls the Evening Chime	138
Far O'er the Deep Blue Sea	137
Farewell to Grog	218
Farragut	210
Father and I Went Down to Camp (Yankee Doodle)	69
Father, Look Up and See that Flag	79
Flag, The American	95
Flag, Float Beautiful, Tho' the War Cry is O'er	142
Flag, God Save Our	9
Flag, Hats Off as the, Goes By	230
Flag, Our, is There	20
Flag of Our Union	22
Flag of the Constellation	36
Flag, Proud, of My Country	89
Flag, The Starry, Floats Free	229
Flag, Stand by the	94
Flag, The Ocean-Guarded, of Light	229
For England, when, with Fav'ring Gale	115
Foretop Morality	183
Freedom of the Seas, The	34
From Aloft the Sailor Looks Around	186
From Erie's Proudly Swelling Breast	201

G

God Save the Flag	9
God Save Our President	55
Go Patter to Lubbers and Swabs, D'ye See	90

H

Hail, Columbia!	5
Hail to the Heroes whose Triumphs have Brighten'd	194

Hark to the Voiceful Anthem	78
Hats Off as the Flag Goes By	230
Heaving the Lead	115
He Leaped in His Boat as it Lay upon the Strand	126
Helmsman's Song, The	189
Here, a Sheer Hulk, Lies Poor Tom Bowling	113
Hero of Erie, The	200
Hornet and the *Peacock*, The	43, 58
How Dashingly in Sun and Light	17
How Gallantly our Battleship	98
How Sleep the Brave who Sink to Rest	66
Hurra! Along the Foaming Tide	178
Hurrah! I'm Off to Sea	145
Hurrah for the Sea	180
Hurrah for the White, Red, and Blue	81

I

Idle, as Though a Painted Ocean	150
If Tars of their Money are Lavish	168
I Have Roamed over Mountain, I've Crossed over Flood	76
In a Little Blue Garment, all Ragged and Torn	163
I Remember the Night was Stormy and Dark	143
It Blew Great Guns when Gallant Tom	147
It Oft Times has been Told (The *Constitution* and the *Guerriere*)	119
It was a Tall Young Oysterman (The Ballad of the Oysterman)	67
It's when Young Men come Home at Night	155
"I've heard," cried out one, "that you Tars tack and tack,"	187

J

Jack Dances and Sings	173
Jackets of Blue, The	232
Jack Ratlin was the Ablest Seaman	167
Jack Steadfast and I were both Messmates at Sea	89
Jolly Sailor Bold	155

K

Kearsarge and *Alabama*	204
Kingdom Coming	227

L

	PAGE
Land and Sea Victories	25
Land of Liberty, The	226
Larboard Watch	212
Liberty Tree	54
Life of a Tar, The	121
Lightly may the Boat Row	131
Long Live America	93
Loud Roared the Dreadful Thunder (Bay of Biscay, O!)	136

M

Maltese Boat Song, The	128
My Bounding Bark, I Fly to Thee	129
My Country, 'tis of Thee (America)	8
My Love is a Sailor and Ploughs the Salt Sea	147
My Love's a Vessel Trim and Gay	188
My Own Native Land	76

N

Nation's Heritage, The	10
Navy, The (When Fame Shall Tell)	57
Navy, Our (Huzza for the Wars!)	233
Navy, Our (On Wings of Glory)	222
Navy, Serving in the	193
Noble Republic! Happiest of Lands	80
Not England's Daughters, Rosy Cheeked	92
Now Coil up Your Nonsense 'bout England's Great Navy	60
Now Smiling Friends and Shipmates all (To Adm'l Farragut)	19

O

Ocean Hero, The	97
O'er the Bosom of Erie (Battle of Lake Erie)	207
O'er the Trident of Neptune	18
O'er the Rough Main with Flowing Sheet	105
Off, off, said the Stranger, Off, off, and Away	164
Of us Tars 'tis Reported Again and Again	175
Oh, Columbia the Gem of the Ocean (Red, White, and Blue)	73

	PAGE
Oh! Calmly may the Waves Flow	131
Oh! Come with Me, My Love	146
O! Pilot, 'tis a Fearful Night	149
Oh! Swiftly Glides the Bonny Boat	127
One Night Came on a Hurricane (Barney Buntline)	148
O! Say Can You See by the Dawn's Early Light (Star-Spangled Banner)	6
On Board the *Cumberland*	38
On the Briny Ocean, O!	13
Our Bark was Out far, far from Land	160
Our Country's our Ship	75
Our Flag is There	20
Our Man-of-War	98
Our Navy	222, 233
Our Sailors and our Ships	17
Our Yankee Ships in Fleet Career	215

P

Paul Jones	28, 105, 110, 139
Phantom Ship, The	154
Pillar of Glory, The	194
Pilot, The	162
Ply the Oar, Brother, and Speed the Boat	143
Poor Bessy was a Sailor's Bride	144
Poor Jack	90
President, God Save Our	55
Proud Flag of My Country! All Gallantly Streaming	89

R

Red, White, and Blue	73
Reefing the Breakers	83
Remember the *Maine*	239
Rise, Columbia, Brave and Free	195
Row Gently Here, My Gondolier	157

S

Sailor, The	215
Sailor's Bequest, The	177

	PAGE
Sailor Boy, Sailor Boy, Sleep my Sweet Fellow	151
Sailor's Grave, The	160
Sailor's Last Whistle, The	122
Sailor's Pride, The	85
Sailor's Tear, The	126
Sailor's Welcome Home, The	130
Sea and Land Victories	25
Seaman's Lay, The	216
Serving in the Navy	193
See, Brother, see how the Night Comes on (Maltese Boat Song)	128
Ship of State, The	21
Stand by the Flag, its Folds have Streamed in Glory	94
Stand to Your Guns, my Hearts of Oak	116, 177
Starry Flag Floats Free, The	229
Star-Spangled Banner	6
Stormy Petrel, The	192
Sweet Goddess That Guides Us	236
Sweetheart, Goodbye	219
Sweet Poll, Adieu	160

T

	PAGE
Tacking Ship off Fire Island Light	208
The Alarmed Skipper	65
The American Boy	79
The American Sailor	61
The American Star	77
The American Tar	95
The Ballad of the Oysterman	67
The Banner of Freedom High Floated Unfurled	223
The Banner of the Sea	235
The Banner of the Stars	56
The Boatswain Calls, the Wind is Fair	171
The *Brandywine*	227
The Busy Crew their Sails Unbending	166
The *Constellation* and the *Insurgente*	53
The *Constitution* and *Guerriere*	63
The *Cumberland*	22
The *Enterprise* and the *Boxer*	221
The Fight was O'er, and Strew'd Around	177
The Freedom of the Seas	34

	PAGE
The Frigate *Constitution*	85
The Gallant Ship was Under Weigh	160
The Goddess of Freedom	95
The Hardy Sailor Braves the Ocean	185
The Heart Knows Only One	179
The Heart that Can Feel for Another	89
The Hero of Erie	200
The *Hornet* and the *Peacock* (Ye Sons of Columbia)	58
The *Hornet* and the *Peacock*, or Victory No. 5	43
The Jackets of Blue	232
The Land of Liberty	226
The Larboard Leech of the Topsail Lines	83
The Larboard Watch	212
The Life of a Tar is the Life I Love	121
The Lighthouse	181
The Mid-Watch	184
The Moon is Beaming Brightly, Love	137
The Moon on the Ocean was Dim'd by a Ripple	112
The Nation's Heritage	10
The Navy (When Fame Shall Tell)	57
The Night was Spent in Mirth and Glee	85
The Ocean Hero	97
The Pillar of Glory	194
The Pilot	162
The Return of the Admiral	190
The Sailor	213
The Seaman's Lay	216
The Sea, the Sea, the Open Sea	156
The Scene was more Beautiful far to my Eye	138
The Ship of State	21
The Signal to Engage shall be	182
The Stormy Petrel	192
The Stripe and the Star	109
The Topsails Shiver in the Wind	235
The True Yankee Statesman	87
The Union, Boys, it is our Birthright	82
The *United States* and *Macedonian*	45, 223
The *Varuna*	205
The Wandering Sailor Ploughs the Main	184
The *Wasp's* Frolic	220
The Wave for Me	235

	PAGE
The Wave of Old Ocean's the Field of the Brave	16
The Yankee Girls	92
The Yankee Man-of-War ('Tis of a Gallant Yankee Ship)	28
The Yankee Man-of-War (We Ride Head to Wind)	217
The Yankee Tar no Danger Knows	121
Then Farewell My Trim-Built Wherry	135
This Life, Boys, at Best's but a Rough Sort of Trip	68
This Life is a Troubled Sea	180
'Tis Said we Vent'rous Die-Hards	170
'Tis the Deed of the Brave	198
Though Lost to Sight, to Memory Dear	219
Though Many and Bright are the Stars that Appear	88
Though Mountains High the Billows Roll	174
Truxton's Victory	37
'Twas Midnight Dark	154
'Twas Saturday Night, the Twinkling Stars	169
'Twas One Morn when the Wind from the Northward Blew Keenly	124
Two Real Tars whom Duty Call'd	183

U

Union and Liberty	82
United States and *Macedonian*	45, 223

V

Varuna, The	205
Viva l'America	80

W

Wake, Sons of Columbia	97
Washington's Grave	83
Wasp's Frolic, The	220
Washed in the Blood of the Brave and the Blooming (God Save the Flag)	9
We are Coming, Father Abra'am	206
We Ride Head to Wind	217
We Sail'd to and fro—on Erie's Broad Lake	103
We Tars have a Maxim	117
When a Boy, Harry Bluff	134

	PAGE
Whene'er the Tyrants of the Main	13
When Fame Shall Tell the Splendid Story	57
When Freedom First the Triumph Sung	195
When Freedom from Her Mountain Height	95
When Freedom's Star Its Last Bright Gleam	11
When Freshly Blows the Northern Gale	189
When First at Sea the Sailor Lad	130
When 'Tis Night and the Midwatch is Come	184
Where Lordly Champlain on its Wild Surging Wave	109
Whether Sailor or Not, for a Moment Avast	122
While Up the Shrouds the Sailor Goes	165
Will Watch	124
Wilt Thou Tempt the Waves With Me?	141
Would'st Thou Know, My Lad, Why Every Tar	161
Would you Know the Ingredients that make up a Tar?	176

Y

Yankee Chronology	49
Yankee Doodle	69
Yankee Doodle, No. 2	72
Yankee Girls, The	92
Yankee Man-of-War, The	28, 217
Yankee Sailors have a Knack	125
Yankee Thunders	46
Ye Gallant Sons of Liberty	72
Ye Honest Tars of Yankee Mould	61
Ye Parliament of England	51
Ye Seamen of Columbia	24
Ye Sons of Columbia	196

www.ingramcontent.com/pod-product-compliance
Lightning Source LLC
Chambersburg PA
CBHW031729230426
43669CB00007B/298